The Mommy Chronicles

The Mommy Chronicles
Leslie Tonner

OPEN ROAD
INTEGRATED MEDIA
NEW YORK

All rights reserved, including without limitation the right to reproduce this book or any portion thereof in any form or by any means, whether electronic or mechanical, now known or hereinafter invented, without the express written permission of the publisher.

Copyright © 1986 by Leslie Tonner

ISBN 978-1-4976-3865-5

This edition published in 2014 by Open Road Integrated Media, Inc.
345 Hudson Street
New York, NY 10014
www.openroadmedia.com

*To Charlie
and
to Charlie's Daddy*

Acknowledgements

With deepest thanks to Wendy Levey, director, and the parents, teachers, and children of the Epiphany Community Nursery School, New York City

Contents

CONFESSIONS OF A ROTTEN MOMMY

Charlie and His Rotten Mommy..1
The Rotten Mommy Refuses to Take Advantage..............................3
Charlie Loves TV...5
Television Commercials That Charlie Likes to Sing........................7
Television Commercials That Charlie Has
Got All Screwed Up in Spite of Billion-
Dollar Ad Campaigns..8
Who, Me???? Wet????...9
My Son the Garbage Truck...11
Bringing It In for under a Thou; or Happy
Birthday, Mommy, You Tightwad..13
Of Human Bondage...16
Charlie the Late Bloomer..18

IF I FORGET THEE, O BANKIE, AND OTHER FAMILY MEMBERS

"And Now, Heeeeere's Bankie!"..23
Ghostbustards..25
The Blended Hostile Nuclear Family..27
"Daddy Says . . ."..29
Take Me Out to the Ball Game...31
Interfacing with Grandma...32
Medieval and Renaissance Children...34
You-Bed..36
Items from Our Floors...38

NATURE ABHORS A VACUUM

Toys R Not Us..43
Jack and Jill Went up the Hill to Fetch a
Container of Häagen-Dazs..45
What Your Stroller Says about You..47
Charlie and Mommy among the Yuckies.......................................49
T-Shirts and Bibs Seen in the Windows of
Ben's for Kids on the Upper East Side
of New York City..51
Prenatal Prep..52

My Baby—A Keepbook for the Eighties...54
The Birthday Brigade..57
Best Looking, Wittiest, Most Likely to
Succeed...59
Item from Our Catalogue..61

A JUG OF WINE, A LOAF OF BREAD, AND A THREE-YEAR-OLD SINGING IN THE WILDERNESS

"I'll Just Pick"..64
Chinese Bones..67
Eat to Win...69

IT'S ONLY YOUR ENTIRE FUTURE HANGING IN THE BALANCE (NURSERY SCHOOL IN THE YEAR TWO)

Charlie (and Mommy) Go to Nursery School....................................73
Charlie and Mommy Continue to Go to
 Nursery School 75
Mommy Goes to Charlie's Teacher Conference.................................77
Charlie Goes to Harvard (Someday)..79
Status Snacks..81
Typhoid Mommy...83
Charlie and Mommy Get Promoted..87

THE TODDLER NETWORK

My Dentist Is My Best Friend..89
Chatting Up the Caregiver.. 91
Sundays, Mondays, Tuesdays, Wednesdays,
 Thursdays, Fridays, and Saturdays in
 the Park with George, Marissa,
 Alessandra, Evan, Courtenay, and
 Jason..93
Contents of Typical Stroller Bag..97

DO YOU CONSIDER A BOX OF PAMPERS CARRY ON LUGGAGE?

The Wings of Boy..101
Bermuda Shorts...103
Wish You Were Here...106
Hamptons Diary by Charlie...107

BROKEN GROWNUPS

Half a Mil and We'll Throw in the Kid..111
Big Bird on My Back..115
Charlie Takes a Meeting..117
The Littlest Prince..120

SESAME STREET AS A METAPHOR FOR LIFE

And That's the Way It Is..124
A Generation of Social Workers..126
White Flight..128
The Official Rotten Mommy Test..131
Afterword: Do Daddies Make the Best
 Mommies? by Charlie's Daddy...134

The Mommy Chronicles

Confessions of a Rotten Mommy

Charlie and his Rotten Mommy

I am a Rotten Mommy. I confess, you don't have to drag it out of me. And because I'm a Rotten Mommy, I set a terrible example for my son. One day I know the other Mommies are going to say, "Why do you want to play with Charlie? He's such a rotten kid!"

To wit. The Mommies are on the March, going out for pizza together. Companionable. Nice. But what does the Rotten Mommy do? She gets a soda for herself and Charlie. The other children, who never have soda, are turned into screaming Coke freaks. It's tantrum city. Mommy and Charlie sit by, sipping their Tab. "Did I cause this?" I ask politely. "Well," I'm told, "they've never had soda in their entire lives!"

Oh. First time ever. And it's all my fault.

But we're not talking about carbonated beverages. This is much more complicated. We're entering the realm of what has come to be known as Sugar Treats (or Sugar Snacks) by the Good Mommies. (A word here about Mominology. You don't say "babysitter" anymore. Uh-uh. You call them caregivers, or caretakers. A cookie or a piece of candy or even a humble graham cracker is known as a sugar treat.)

I allow Charlie to have these things. Not steadily, I'm no idiot, but if he wants them, okay, let it be. The other Mommies look on these things as Unclean. Their children nibble Rice Cakes and other items that look like mattress stuffing. They also eat gobs of raisins that stick to the teeth, but never mind. I don't argue with Other Mommies. Except one day when a mother in a toddler group I'm in picked up an entire tin of Danish butter cookies and announced she was "getting rid" of this abomination. "Now wait a minute." I growled. And everyone stared at me. Not throw out a cookie? Are you a real Mommy or what?

And it doesn't stop there. One Mommy politely inquired if I had ever fed my firstborn son a h-o-t d-o-g. "Oh, you mean a hot dog," I said, mentioning the Unmentionable. "Sure. All the time. Whenever he wants. Hebrew National."

Kosher isn't good enough for the Mommies. They want nitrite-free stuff from the expensive butcher on Third Avenue. I am reduced to feeling like a heel and can only envision the day when Charlie shocks the pants off some nice Mommy by asking for (gasp!) a hot dog, a Coke, and some cookies for lunch, please, hold the rice cakes. A rotten kid.

The Rotten Mommy Refuses to Take Advantage

Living in New York City stinks, particularly if you've got a small kid. What are you seeing every day, for instance, that's improving him as a person? Bums sleeping on gratings with empty wine bottles? Old men exposing themselves right in front of the pizzeria? Two guys in leather jackets exchanging cash for pills in your vest-pocket park? (Do you think it's called vest pocket because that's where they stash the stuff?) Garbage?

As a matter of fact, Charlie *loves* garbage, because he seriously believes Oscar lives in metal trash cans, and he loves garbage trucks more than he does his grandparents, his sister, or his astonishing collection of little metal cars. I suppose it's educational, watching garbagemen throw the stuff into the back of the truck, but I'll let that pass for now.

We're talking here about culture, and New York City offers plenty. So it's no surprise that Mommies have taken it upon themselves to cancel out all that city sleaze with Things Uplifting. Problem is if you don't indulge, your sense of Rotten Mommyhood grows proportionately.

The Mommies *do* a lot. Charlie's contemporaries go to Ice Capades, the circus (Big Apple *and* Ringling, guys), the movies (Disney retreads as well as commercial tie-ins), the Metropolitan Museum, the Museum of the City of New York, the Guggenheim, and I could go on and on, but you get the picture. I even know one father who took a five-year-old to see Boito's *Mefistofele* at City Opera, but that's another story. I can only tell you about Toddler Mommies.

Charlie is deprived. We don't do a whole lot of that stuff, mainly because I resent paying money to watch Charlie have a tantrum during the first act of *The Nutcracker* because he's tired and hungry. I figure I can get to see that at my local D'Agostino's free. So when they tell me they're going to the Sesame Street Sky Show at the Hayden Planetarium and then on to the Museum of Natural History to catch the *To Fly* movie, I say, "Yes. We've been to the Natural History already." Then I yawn. We actually did take him there, once. Two minutes for the dinosaur bones, two minutes for the dioramas, two minutes for the gems, etc. Real Olympic records set here. And we are going to go back. Sometime.

When they ask me if I've taken Charlie to the Museum of Broadcasting yet, I reply, "We prefer Natural History. The dioramas are *so* educational."

Am I taking him to the Medieval Fair at the Cloisters? "Natural History is his place," I say earnestly. "We're studying the Eskimos now."

I suppose the guilt will get to me and he'll get older and ask and then we'll go to everything, but right now I am glad I don't have to leave *The Nutcracker* after the first ten minutes because it's clear he doesn't want to sit in his forty-five dollar seat, and I don't miss being in twenty-degree weather trying to focus his concentration for 120 sustained seconds on the Bullwinkle balloon in Macy's Thanksgiving Day Parade. He doesn't even know who Bullwinkle is. And all of this just makes me an even Rottener Mommy.

Charlie Loves TV

You've heard it all before. The kids love *Sesame Street*. The first word they say is "Grover." They can keep Bert and Ernie straight (isn't Ernie the one with the stupid laugh and the pigeons? Or is that Bert?). They are sophisticated about Big Bird's fears and Oscar's kvetching. They watch the show day after day. Savvy New York City mothers know that by parlaying the PBS showings of S.S. on local and cable channels, they can get a cool five hours of the show into the kid each weekday. And that ain't bad, especially when you're talking windchill of ten below or better.

But let's leave all that Jim Henson stuff aside and talk about Charlie in the big world—the world of Network TV. Charlie and Prime Time. You're not supposed to let your kid watch, right? It's finger paints and puzzles and Where's Spot all the time, right? Well, let me be the first to admit it. I let my kid Watch.

And watch he does. Charlie's seen about half of *Jewel in the Crown*, one-third of *King Lear*, and selected moments of Wagner's *Ring* cycle. His adolescent sister lets him watch sitcoms. But it's with Mommy that he really turns on to his faves.

Charlie loves what he calls *Goldfish News*. What is this entity, you ask?

Anything like *Monty Python?* Don't tell Charlie, but this is actually ABC's *World News Tonight*. Their twirling globe reminds my son of a goldfish bowl. You tell him *Goldfish News*, and he'll sing you their theme song. "Dah dah dah dah-h-h, dah dah dah dah dah dah!" He grins proudly. Congratulations and go to Horace Mann, kid.

The next treat is his favorite, favorite show, known in this household as *Tainment Night*, a.k.a. *Entertainment Tonight*, and this theme song he'll sing with great enthusiasm and emphasis. He sings it *better* than he sings "Wheels on the Bus," and that's saying a lot. He is famous here for describing the anchorwoman on the show as wearing a dress made of sprinkles (sequins).

After *Tainment Night* it's all downhill.

But this must be said. Charlie is not a television zombie. He actually does *watch*. Night after night, famine, pestilence, plague, Bhopal, Ethiopia, plane crashes, fires, scandals, terrorism, he takes it all in. He listens. And he asks questions. "Whassat?" he says, pointing at a tractor-trailer rig that has jacknifed and caused a thirty-two-car pileup on some interstate. "Itssa, itssa, itssa truck," he bursts out triumphantly. "It's broken."

Television Commercials that Charlie Likes to Sing

NBC Let's All Be There!
We're American Airlines, Something Special in the Air
You'll See How Good It Can Be at Your Ford Dealers
 Right Now
Pick, Pick, Pick (Perdue Oven Stuffer Roasters)
Crispy Chewy (Duncan Hines Cookies)
Who Says You Can't Have It All? (Michelob Light)

Television Commercials that Charlie has got All Screwed Up in Spite of Billion-Dollar Ad Campaigns

A nything with Ronald McDonald, whom Charlie thinks is Old McDonald on his farm (It's a good time for the great taste . . . Old McDonald's.)

Who, Me???? Wet????

Don't mention toilet training in our house. Banish "potty" from your vocabulary. Substitute "diaper" and "changing table." Underwear, no. In fact, never.

We have a little problem here. Yes, I know that boys are supposed to be harder to train. Look, harder to train still implies trainable. How about not trainable, Dr. Spock? How about "We Shall Not Be Moved," Dr. Brazelton? How about forget it, Charlie?

The problem is simply that my son has schooled himself in the simple approach of deny, deny, deny. If you ask him if he's wet, he'll say, "No. I dry." Or "I pretty dry," getting into Advanced Comparative Denial.

You can try asking the more serious question, but the results are the same. "Did you make a doody?" you ask. "No," he says, shaking his head violently. "I dry." Try telling him that it's obvious to everyone on the sixth floor of our apartment building that he's made a ca-ca, and he'll hang on to his story. He's developing skills that will enable him to become (a) a great divorce attorney, (b) Richard Nixon, or (c) the consigliere of a great Mafioso family.

His innocent and rather earnest reactions to our queries have resulted in a more aggressive inquiring policy in our house. To determine if he needs changing, we never ask, we just grab the kid and stick our hands inside. This occurs while Charlie is still protesting (loudly), "I dry! I dry!" Yeah, sure.

When Charlie attended a school summer program this past June, I had to rely on the fortitude of others to carry on our Crusade. "You gotta change him," I explained, handing over a supply of Pampers. At the end of Day One, he was the only kid still dressed in his bathing suit. "Where are his shorts?" I asked, thinking that they must have had an afternoon at the sprinklers in the park and forgotten to change him.

"Uh, he had a little accident. His shorts got really wet."

I didn't understand. A little accident is what you say about them when they're toilet training. "When did you change him?"

The teacher, looking harried, wrinkled her brow. "We asked him all morning if he was wet, and he told us he was dry."

HE TOLD THEM HE WAS DRY! AND THEY BELIEVED HIM!!

Now when people inquire if my little boy is toilet-trained, I have only one reply. "Don't ask."

My Son the Garbage Truck

Charlie tells people that when he grows up, "I going to be a garbage truck."

He means it.

People always smile indulgently and gently correct him. "Oh, you mean a garbage*man*." When that notion registers, they add faintly, "That's nice."

"No, no," we correct them. "He means a garbage *truck*. He wants to be a truck."

Charlie loves garbage trucks. They make wonderful noises. A whole bunch of them line up outside his windows, no doubt on their garbage truck coffee break, and he counts them one by one. He loves their attendant "brush trucks," as he calls them, that sweep the street. He especially loves to watch the trucks eat the garbage. He'll sit for long minutes studying the process and imitating the noise. I guess if you want to be one, you have to know how.

His favorite Matchbox toy is his sanitation truck. Ditto Corgi. His favorite *Sesame Street* character is Oscar the Grouch in the garbage can. Charlie walks down the street and knocks on every can calling, "Hi, Oscar, you in there?" Then he lowers his voice and replies, gruffly, "Go away!"

He has made his tricycle into a garbage truck. Every night, collected on the rear running board, are Charlie's garbage gleanings: little bits of carpet fluff, stray paper clips, crumbs, chewed gum, and other detritus.

He had one bad moment with all this when a kindly gentleman, meaning well, shook his head as Charlie announced his life's ambition.

"Surely you don't want to be a garbage truck!" he said with a manner like a high school guidance counselor telling a senior that of course he didn't want to go to Miami U., there were *better* schools. "It's a dirty kind of truck," he went on. "You don't want to be such a dirty truck, do you?"

Charlie was crestfallen. He didn't answer right away. After the man left us, Charlie looked up at me. "No," he said firmly, "I going to be a clean garbage truck."

Well, Miami U. does get nice weather, and he could learn to surf, and he'd be near his grandma . . .

Bringing it in for Under a Thou, or Happy Birthday, Mommy, you Tightwad

The subject of the toddler birthday party has been discussed ad nauseum; everyone has heard of the theme birthday parties (Pirates á Go-Go, Turtle Wedding, Nonviolent Forest Creatures Peacefully Coexist, and so on). The clown and puppeteer route has been traveled so frequently that the kids can bawl out the punch lines in unsion. It's a little like caterers in the eighties; people who go to a dinner party catered by Mr. X know exactly what to expect in terms of menu, style, presentation, and sexual orientation of waiters and bartenders. Similarly, well-partied tykes have seen it All.

Thus the return to the Old-Fashioned Inexpensive Party we remember from our unjaded youths. I never saw the likes of paid professional entertainment at my childhood parties. The most you could hope for was somebody's father screwing up the home movies and cursing out his cumbersome camera equipment.

So it was with Great Expectations that I planned Charlie's third birthday party and decided to go for Reverse Snobbism; I'd do the party the way we did parties in my day, and maybe instead of looking like a cheapskate, I'd start a new Trend. At this moment *New York Magazine* still hasn't called, but I'm hopeful.

Here's how it worked, broken down by expenses:

PROVISIONS FOR SIX CHILDREN

Hats (discontinued Sesame *Street variety*,
half-price at neighborhood store) $ 1.75

Napkins (ditto hats, half-price) $ .60

(A word must be inserted here about the current unfashionability of Sesame Street and Smurf items. While the TV shows are still going strong and children this age can identify the characters with trust and love, the biggies in napkins, party hats, and the like seem to be Masters of the Universe, Rainbow Brite, and Mr. T. I've been telling Charlie that his father is Master of the Universe, since it helps to get him to bed on time, but the napkins, etc., imply otherwise. We'll have to stay tuned for further developments in the paper party goods area for the final word on this.)

Apple juice, store brand (less coupon) $ 1.00

Funny-looking plastic drinking
    straws that curl around like
    pretzels (double as party favor) $ 2.00

Plastic cups (out of much larger
    package, cost approximate)   .25

Plates that say Happy Birthday $ 1.25

Bubble stuff (wand in the bottle)
    for 6, 49¢ each $ 2.94
Yankee Doodle cupcakes successfully
    disguised with a handful of sprinkles
    and the addition of some candles to
    look like homemade cake (1 dozen) $ 1.95

Six Häagen-Dazs ice cream cups (a true extravagance but Dolly Madison
    cups not sold on the Upper East Side) $ 3.60

                        TOTAL $15.34

                 COST PER CHILD $ 2.5566666

This affair was pronounced "chic" by the Mommies, and the children had an excellent time.

But here's the rub: Charlie and his ilk are fairly oblivious to the content of these parties. They don't care what's happening, it's the Mommies who care and who compare one party with another. But as the kids get older, their own demands will increase. Next year it'll be a different story. Charlie will want Masters of the Universe, no doubt, and this time he won't mean Daddy.

Of Human Bondage

MOST parents share fond memories of their child's firsts—the first word said, first step taken, first haircut, first birthday. We on the other hand remember an even more remarkable first, one that my husband often says separates a child from an uncivilized denizen of the jungle: the first time he fetched.

As this criterion is the strictest test of a child's amiability and good nature, it might behoove those folks who produce baby books to list fetching among "Baby's First Activities." It's a far more useful trait to learn than walking and talking. Once they start walking and talking, you can't get them to stop.

Here are a few tips about how to instill the essential character trait of fetching in your child:

- First, make sure your child understands specifically what you want him to do. DO NOT SAY, "Charlie, go get me my lunch." DO SAY, "Charlie, please hand me that turkey sandwich from the refrigerator." BETTER STILL, start a system of early training and rewards, i.e., "Charlie, how would you like some delicious turkey sandwich? You would? Then here's what you do. . . ."

- Start small. We weaned Charlie on little asks. Getting the newspaper, for instance, is not a great idea because if it's the Sunday *Times*, the kid gets a hernia and you get your "Classified Ads" mixed up with "Arts and Leisure." Bringing you a simple napkin or tray of canapés is a much better bet. By the age of four you can start on the Sunday paper provided it's a slim holiday weekend edition.

- Key some tasks into the kid's life-style. Teach him to bring you the stuff he wants. A cookie? He can get the package. A puzzle? He can go pick it out. A pizza? He can phone up for it.

- Say, "Please" and "Thank you." DO NOT SAY, "Fetch." You'll confuse the dog.

Get your fetching in while you can; once your child enters preadolescence (which in today's youngsters can begin as early as six and a half), it's all over. Many people plan their second children to fill in the fetching gap. Spacing three or four years apart isn't bad, though there may be a critical few months during which you will have to fetch for yourself.

Finally, here are a few homilies to get you through that period of time when the kid starts asking, "Why?" to everything. Invoke one of the following when appointing tasks: "The Lord helps those who help their parents." "Honor thy father and thy mother." "Remember the neediest." "Mr. T (or Rainbow Brite or Barbie or whoever) got started this way!"

Charlie the Late Bloomer

Late blooming is the scourge of the eighties. God forbid your child does not do something On Time, let alone Early. Conscientious mothers begin their push-ahead fantasies while pregnant; labors are dutifully compared ("I spent *two hours* in transition. How long were *you?*"), as are Apgar scores, baby's length and weight, duration of nursing, and first stool.

I have done my own share of bragging. When Charlie got to his feet and walked at the age of exactly eleven months, I contemplated hiring a sound truck to cruise the neighborhood. You see, blooming ahead of schedule is equated with genius. Never mind that Albert Einstein didn't talk until age four and that his mother today would have him in therapy; today's Einstein counts backward by age two, in Spanish by age two and a half, and calculates the square footage of your co-op by age three.

All of this is to introduce the confession that my son is, to my great dismay, a Late Bloomer. Yes, he's a boy, I know they mature later and all that, but that doesn't explain why Charlie is a Late-Blooming Terrible Two.

Even non-parents know about this famous phase when children throw tantrums, say No! to everything, give their parents a constant hard time, and generally make themselves pains in the asses. Charlie was an okay Terrible

Two, a lot better than most, and so when this negative stuff seemed to abate near his third birthday, we breathed a collective sigh of relief. "That wasn't so bad," we congratulated each other.

Not so fast.

As soon as the magic Third passed, a transformation came over my son. He entered the Latent Terrible Twos, which we were not prepared for, and which my child-rearing books do not give a fancy name. We were left high and dry. Afraid to ask other parents if their children suffered the same problem, we had to settle for the disheartening fact that just maybe we had given birth to a Late Bloomer and that what we were facing at the age of three was, in fact, last year's leftover behavior. It's like having your kid repeat a grade in school; there's no getting around the embarrassment.

Each day, as we try to cope with the defiance, the tantrums, the foot-stamping, head-shaking, general nuisance making, we try to look ahead to the future. What other surprises are in store for us that nobody told us about? After the Horrible Threes are we going to get hit with the Revolting Fours and the Truly Disgusting Fives?

I am suspicious about Charlie being the only Late Bloomer of this ilk; don't all Mommies and Daddies fib a bit to protect the image of their young? Perhaps I've identified a *Trend* (and wouldn't that look nice on Charlie's nursery school résumé? Trend setter). So here's a little quiz to see if your child, too, is a secret Late Bloomer. All answers will be kept strictly confidential and will not become part of your child's Permanent School Record. I promise.

Score 5 points for each Yes, zero for a No

1. Does your child think you are Dr. Mengele if you try to get him to brush his teeth?

2. Is the most expensive item your child has intentionally broken worth more than $150, and are you still paying it off on your MasterCard? (Add 5 points if it was a priceless family heirloom.)

3. Has your child ever brought to a halt the activities of five hundred people or more (at Shea Stadium, for example) by the decibel level of his shrieking? (Add 5 points if glass was broken, subtract 10 if you intentionally pinched him to get him to scream so you could smuggle your new Rolex through customs.)

4. Have you ever been sued by the parents of another child (and did the scars eventually fade)?

5. What's the worst injury your child has inflicted on you: scratched cornea (2 points), broken bone (5 points), perfect impression of full set of toddler teeth on forearm (10 points, plus 5 if you got an infection)?

What your score means:

    0-10:   Congratulations. You are successfully raising an Airedale and are finding "No More Bad Dogs" a lot more helpful than Lee Salk. Keep up the good work.

    10-25:   Your kid is a Late Bloomer Manqué. Get it straight with your self how awful you want him to be and Follow Through.

    25 points +:   You may have the next Einstein on your hands. Increase your liability coverage and smile. Figure out what you'd like to wear to the Nobel Prize Awards Ceremony (nothing low-cut, please).

If I forget thee, O Bankie, and Other Family Members

"And Now, Heeeeere's Bankie!"

Call me Bankie.
    Bankie is THE blanket of choice, the one we all had as kids that trailed behind us, got increasingly smelly, grungy, and unraveled, and eventually dissolved into a handful of dust. Good-bye, and amen.

Bankie, too, started out as a lovely yellow Saks Fifth Avenue Baby Boutique item. But now we are all hard-pressed to recall the satin binding, long gone, or the pale color, now converted to dinge.

The interesting thing about Bankie is that only one corner of it serves as Charlie's focal point, and this is, of course, the stinkiest, vilest part of all. This corner has been dubbed by its owner, "Seewah." Why Seewah? Who knows? Why did God choose to call the first man Adam? Why did Frank Zappa call his kids Moon Unit and Dweezil?

In our household Charlie's security blanket has thus become a fashionable hyphenate: Bankie-Seewah. "Anyone seen Bankie-Seewah?" "Would you make sure to put Bankie-Seewah in the wash?" and so on.

Charlie clearly understands the magical principle behind Seewah; when he's tired, hurt, blue, or cranky, he'll call for his Bankie corner to comfort him. It's the equivalent of taking a shot of brandy, or a Valium, I suppose, only this tranquilizer is fraying and operates manually. Seewah is picked up, placed near the thumb that Charlie sucks, and flapped gently as it is applied to his mouth, nose, and occasionally his ear.

Seewah is a transferable commodity as well. If you're having a bad day, are sick, tired, or have hurt yourself, Charlie will approach you with his fraying blanket end and inquire politely, "Want some Seewah?"

And clearly my son believes that we live in a Bankie-Seewah world. While watching a Charlie Brown special one night, he grew ecstatic at the sight of Linus. "Look, look," he pointed. "The little boy has a Seewah."

Considering the fact that the Charlie Brown strip has just turned thirty-five, I shudder to think what Linus's Bankie must smell like by now.

Ghostbustards

Having a teen-age sister is admittedly something of a gas for Charlie. He's the school pet, the class Baby Brother. She puts him on the phone with all her friends. "Say hi to Laura," she prompts. "Hi Wauwaa."

He's a good excuse for not getting homework done ("Charlie hid my math book," "Charlie stole my pen." "Charlie won't let me do my Latin, he wants me to sing 'Baa Baa Black Sheep' with him!"). I'm sure that at school the teachers hear how Charlie ate her homework for dinner. They must think he's a goat.

Very small brothers are an endless source of educational fun, too. You can teach them all sorts of expressions that sound riotous coming out of the mouth of a toddler. Because of Emily, Charlie now knows how to say the following (his version):

> "Gross me out da door!"
> "No wayyyyyyy."
> "Who d'ya call? Ghostbustards."
> "I wanna MTV."
> "Whassa matter, Doc?"

Charlie also has to suffer the fate of being a large, living doll. Emily likes to dress him up and do his hair. He comes running in to show off his new coiffures, pinned back with barrettes and hairbands or pulled atop his head with plastic, neon-colored clips. Next thing I know she'll try to dress him up like Madonna.

Such a ten-year age gap leaves an older sister in the role of part mother, part aunt, part caretaker, and part comforter. Charlie is "my baby" to Emily as much as he's our baby. But what we've learned from their relationship is that no amount of years can change or alter the love. The house rings with the sound of Charlie happily calling for his sister on the days she's with us, "Amawee, Amawee!" It's one of the nicest sounds I know.

The Blended Hostile Nuclear Family

The reason they call it a nuclear family is because its potential is so explosive. And with so many divorces today, you've got a situation resembling a lot of minicyclotrons capable of triggering a major atomic disaster.

Ex-wives hover somewhere over the horizon like that cloud of locusts in *The Good Earth* that at any minute is going to swoop down and munch up everything in the field, finally buzzing away and leaving only the husks.

Our family is no different from many—better in some ways, not so good in others. Charlie is too young to understand that his daddy is divorced and that Emily has another home where she lives with her mother. As far as he's concerned, when she leaves here, she's going to school, period. Dark of night, Sundays, summer, it makes no difference. To him it's school.

When he's older, he'll want to know what's going on. How do you explain all this to a toddler?

Late at night I conjure up ways to make divorce understandable. I could describe it as something like "Three Billy Goats Gruff," or "The Three Little Pigs." Perhaps add a touch of "Chicken Licken" and a dab of "Snow White."

I am told that small children adjust to all this information quite well. But how to explain it properly so the adjustment will follow?

Publishers, I'd like to suggest some titles to be added to all Blended Hostile Nuclear Family bookshelves so that future remarried parents don't have to worry about messy explanations. These would include:

Pat the Alimony Check
Where's Spot's Half Sister?
Richard Scarry's Best Divorce Book Ever
A Child's Garden of Lawsuits
Where the Wild Thing Is
The Care Bears Visit Their Noncustodial Parent

"Daddy Says..."

1. Daddy says that germs do not exist and illness is not catching. He is happy to finish Charlie's food, even though Charlie is running a fever of 102 and coughing regularly. Daddy gets lots of colds right after Charlie does. But if you suggest that there might be a relationship here, you are subjected to a lecture on what a stupid concept germs is anyway.

2. Daddy says that southpaws are flakes and no kid of his is going to be a lefty. Charlie is currently ambidextrous but leaning to the right, which is a great relief to Daddy, who is teaching Charlie to bat righty, throw righty, and go to his left.

3. Daddy says that children do not learn by example, so basically it doesn't matter what you do anyway. As a result Charlie has learned to do the following:

    - drink out of bottles without pouring the contents into a glass;
    - verbalize while sneezing (Daddy's favorite sneeze word being

"Habruska"); Charlie has also learned the same trick while burping and yawning;

- eat peanut butter and jelly straight out of their respective jars using one spoon;

- mainline Velveeta.

4. Daddy says that boys have to learn to be independent, and so he lets Charlie climb to the highest part of the jungle gym in the park while he sits on a bench listening to the Mets on his Walkman. Mommy doesn't go to the park with them anymore. Mommy stays home and has a nervous breakdown.

5. Daddy says it's never too soon to begin the sports habit, so Charlie watches the Giants, the Mets, the Masters, the Open, and Wimbledon and identifies each sport correctly. He's still a bit mixed up about what's going on (he is convinced that sliding into home plate is "tackling," for instance, but then so was Thurman Munson).

6. Daddy says encyclopedic knowledge is a good thing, so Charlie knows the name of everything that moves. Recently he corrected the mother of one of his nursery school friends who pointed out a "steam shovel." "'S not a steam shovel, itssa *power* shovel," he said with authority. He was right.

7. Daddy says what he thinks in front of Charlie. So Charlie is growing up convinced that the only Yankees on earth beat the Confederates in a war, that George Foster/Darryl Strawberry/ Rafael Santana, etc., is a bum regardless of Grand Slam homers, RBIs, or other weekly stats, and that Daddies as well as Mommies give baths, cook dinners, and do dishes. Not a bad way to start out in life, notwithstanding habruskas!

Take me Out to the Ball Game

Charlie attends his first Mets game in the company of his father and his grandfather ("Poppa").

ITEMS PURCHASED:

>One official Mets hardball
>One hot dog with ketchup
>Paper cup of french fries with ketchup
>Large Coke
>Boy-sized Mets hat
>Box of popcorn
>Large Coke
>Mets pennant
>Vanilla/chocolate dixie cup
>Mets T-shirt, flaming-orange and blue
>Another large Coke to replace second one, which spilled

FINAL SCORE: Mets 5—Expos 2—Charlie $27.85

Interfacing with Grandma

Charlie has two grandmas. The grandma who's here (in New York) and the grandma who's there (in Florida).

Grandmas have, like everything else, undergone a revolution in the last ten years. First of all, they're generally a bit older, as their kids waited longer to have their own children. But they look younger. Most of them aren't gray anymore. And they exercise and diet, so they're not cozy and plump either. No more aprons and flowered cotton shifts. In fact, they're looking good: coordinated suits and silk blouses, gold earrings and chains, bracelets and Rolex watches, Ferragamo shoes, Clinique makeup. All in all, grandmas are sharp.

Remember how your grandma used to knit you a lumpy scarf and hat to match, which you didn't want to wear because it was made and not bought in a store? Or if your grandma bought you something in a store, she might as well have made it because it was a cardigan with little designs in pearls across the top? Which you never wore, or if you did, you immediately spilled Bosco on it so it would be out of wardrobe circulation for a while?

Forget it. Grandmas don't make stuff anymore. They buy. And when they buy, they buy the right things. They want their grandchildren looking sharp. So from grandmas, Charlie gets Lacoste, Benetton, Absorba, Fusen

Usagi, Adidas, and a flowered print bag from Saks for his early months to tote tushy impedimenta.

And cooking? Remember how grandmas cooked? All that chicken soup with noodles and pot roast and apple strudel? Forget the cooking. Grandmas know their cholesterol levels like grandpas know six-month Treasury Bill rates and they eat spa diets and when they cook it's things like Chicken Piccata and steamed broccoli and hearts of lettuce with a little lemon squeezed on it.

And grandmas don't sit at home and wait for you to visit either. They drop in when they're in the city for a meeting or a matinee, or they call when they're not having a bridge evening or (gasp) out on a date—in short, how is Charlie going to relate to the concept of Grandma?

He'll wonder why Little Red Riding Hood's grandma is in bed with a cap over her gray curls. How come she's not touching up her hair with a rinse at least, and dressed in a jogging suit, and where's Grandma's car and her Fendi bag and what's she doing in that forest when she's supposed to live in a *condo*?

Medieval and Renaissance Children

When addressing myself to the similarities between my three-year-old son and my thirteen-year-old stepdaughter, I often invoke this equation: 3 is to 13 as the Dark Ages is to Western Civilization.

With both children, you discover an amazing number of similarities:

1. *Half the time you can't understand what they're talking about.* Charlie likes to say that "pickles have wings." What does this mean? Similarly, when Emily discusses the merits of Sheila E. versus Madonna, I haven't a clue as to what this is about either.

2. *They do not clean up after themselves.* I find myself picking up off the floor, alternately, Charlie's bristle blocks, Emily's gum wrappers, Charlie's little metal cars (hell on bare feet in the middle of the night), the little backs of Emily's pierced earrings (similar hell on said feet), Charlie's potato chip crumbs, Emily's potato chip crumbs.

3. *There's a wide mood variance that can strike in a matter of moments.* Sunny Charlie

can turn black in an instant. If *Sesame Street* ends and he wants more, it's not good enough to explain that whether he likes it or not, he's going to have to watch *MacNeil-Lehrer* because that's all there is. Emily's adolescent mood swings run a similar gamut, though the reasons for her changes are less obvious and probably hormonal (isn't that what all parents hope?). But if you can imagine a three-year-old in a rotten mood concurrent with that of a thirteen-year-old, you have some idea of how much fun we have in our house!

But what, you ask, does this have to do with the Dark Ages?

You see, having children of these respective ages is like living in Medieval times. Communication is practically nil, literacy is at a low ebb, understanding certainly wanes with each passing day, and culture is all but unidentifiable. Basically you're sitting around waiting for the Renaissance. With a three-year-old, this could be when he starts elementary school and is gone from nine to three; with the thirteen-year-old it should arrive around the time she turns twenty-one.

So here's to Mommy and Daddy, a little like those monks cloistered in the monastery and writing on parchment, preserving what they can of civilization and hoping that the rest of the world will one day tune in and join the human race. Now let's see, 21 minus 13 is 8? Just eight more years? Is that possible . . .?

You-Bed

Charlie is very good at adjectives, passing fair at adverbs, fantastic at nouns, okay at verbs, but not so hot on pronouns.

When Charlie says "you-bed," he means my bed. Got that? Let me run it by you again. You-bed means Mommy and Daddy's bed. The problem is Charlie doesn't yet understand "my bed," so if I want him to go into his bed, I have to say, "Charlie's bed," and if I don't want him in my bed, I have to say, "you-bed." Thus, in the evening I sometimes give him a choice: "Charlie, you can come in you-bed for a while, and then you have to go in Charlie's bed, all right?" "Wanna stay in you-bed," he answers. "You can't go to sleep in you-bed," I answer, extremely careful not to say "my bed" and blow the whole deal.

If Charlie says, "Want you to help me," what he means is *he* wants to help *you*. If I'm making french toast, he'll pull over his chair calling out, "Help me, help me," which means he wants to be sous-chef and help break the eggs and pour in the milk. This can be a bit puzzling, but it's also charming.

If he puts out his arms and cries, "Held, held," he wants you to pick him up.

These little word plays make our kids still small to us. But as other baggage of infancy, such as diapers and bottles and bibs, pass on, so will these misuses. We have bid fond adieu to "backsies cuck" (garbage truck) and "sicka sees" (cottage cheese) and are preparing to part with "locomovis" (locomotive).

We seem to have adopted some of Charlie's baby lingo as a private family way of communicating, though I must admit to feeling there's a teeny bit to be desired when your husband looks at you sexily, raises his eyebrows, and says, "Wanna go to you-bed?"

Items from our Floors

LIVING ROOM:

1 Tomy Folkswagon with Fisher-Price school bus tied to rear to make train
18 bristle blocks, multicolored, spread over 2 yard radius from ground zero
1 copy *Curious George Gets a Medal*
Top of Colorforms Muppet Babies box
Ruler, hammer, and assorted screws from Fisher Price workbench
1 Buddy Mack tow truck
1 Buddy power shovel minus shovel
1 Hasbro cast-iron Big Bird driving convertible
1 Matchbox double-decker British bus
Flatbed trailer, minisized, minus cab
Wiffle bat
1 copy *Richard Scarry's Busiest People Ever*

KITCHEN:

1 walking robot, batteries not included

1 googly-eyed duck hand puppet (never washed) with gaping hole above bill
Tricycle
3 pennies
4 Fisher-Price people (postman, little girl with smile and ponytail, stewardess, ringmaster)
Magnetic letters B, J, and W

DEN:

1 Marx CHIPS motorcycle
1 aviator's cap
1 blue plastic dump truck with 11 Fisher-Price people dumped inside as cargo (including two black-and-white panda dogs, construction workers, pilot, and three cross children with freckles and baseball caps turned to one side)
Pieces of Cap'n Crunch jigsaw puzzle (minus one boot and pirate's chest of gold)
Salt shaker, three plastic plates, and plastic egg from cooking set
Record jacket from "Sesame Street Sing-Along"
Batteries from robot
Green plastic nails from Fisher-Price Work-bench

MASTER BEDROOOM:

Caboose from wooden train with piece chipped off roof
Mattel shopping cart with contents of Mommy's makeup kit spilled inside basket
Charlie's sneakers and one of his socks
Two sticky, empty glasses from apple juice consumed earlier
Crumbs from pretzels that accompanied apple juice
Wiffle ball (under bed)
Broken pieces of chalk
Hess oil truck/bank with batteries missing so lights don't work
Broken cassette of kindergarten fun-time songs
Doll known as Baby less her blue flannel pajamas
Bankie-Seewah
Box of Baby Fresh wipes (half-empty)
Magnetic letters R, V, and D
Charlie's pajamas from previous night

CHARLIE'S ROOM:

Mommy's sneakers
Daddy's socks
$1.87 in change, mainly pennies, nickels, and dimes
More broken chalk
The rest of magnetic alphabet set with L, S, and
 two O's missing
Cap'n Crunch's pirate chest
7 Matchbox and other minisized cars including Rolls Royce, Jaguar,
 Corvette, classic MG, and two garbage trucks
Two framed photos from Mommy's nighttable
Daddy's reading glasses minus case
Spaghetti measure from kitchen wall display
1 bath towel
Charlie

Nature Abhors a Vacuum

Toys R not Us

THERE'S this *obsession* with toys now. It's not enough that they have to be educational and expensive; they have to be made of natural materials and approved by various agencies of the federal government and free of carcinogens and purchasable only in these full-price, out-of-the-way retail establishments with snotty employees.

"Oh, surely you wouldn't want that," the salesperson informs you with a sniff. You take your American-made plastic toy and place it back, guiltily, on the shelf.

"What do you recommend for a three-year-old?" I inquire. This is more intimidating than browsing in Veneziano, I'm starting to think.

She shows me something with writing on it in a foreign language. I realize it's in German. I try to translate. It says something like "fungebrazen." I'm hoping this means that the toy is fun. By carefully studying the color photos, I realize I'm being shown some kind of Young Pasteur set, with junior microscope and petri dishes. Petri dishes? Charlie scarcely plays with his plastic Jack and Jill miniature tea set, complete with rubber doughnut and plastic Nabisco saltine.

"Are you sure this is right for a three-year-old?" I ask timidly. One does not say three-year-old "boy," as we enlightened Mommies, surely, are not sexist. Besides, no one shows you stuff like dolls anymore. They're out.

The bored, upwardly mobile salesperson is scouting the store for a more promising Mommy than me. Perhaps a Mommy with a Carlos Falchi bag and coordinated stockings and Maud Frizon shoes, not this Mommy wreck with her discount Keds.

I slink away and hope she doesn't notice me. The fungebrazen or whatever it's called is $49.95. I settle for a French concrete truck (how do I know it's French? Well, at least I had four years of *that* in high school) with a friction engine and a provenance attached to the box that tells me how sensational this toy is and how much my "enfant" will "aime" it. Great.

The really interesting part is that no matter what I cart home—French trucks, German blocks, Danish puzzles, even Macao Matchbox cars (the new state-of-the-art locale for England's finest), Charlie has one favorite toy in our house. The garlic press.

Jack and Jill went Up the Hill to Fetch a Container of Häagen-Dazs

WHAT'S UPSCALE AND WHAT'S NOT:

Huggies are upscale. Pampers are not.
Häagen-Dazs is upscale. Good Humor is not.
Not watching TV is upscale. Watching is not.
Sneakers are upscale. Shoes are not.
Szechuan is upscale. Spaghetti-Os are not.
One child is upscale. Children are not.
Johnson and Johnson wipes are upscale. Damp toilet paper is not.
Snugli convertible diaper bags with roll-out changing mats are upscale.
Oversized canvas totes that read Le Shopping Bag are not.
Jelly (sandals) are upscale. Jelly (and peanut butter) is not.
Imported bubble stuff with the wand stuck to the cap so you don't have to get your fingers wet trying to fish the stick out is upscale. Regular bubble stuff is not.
Caran d'ache watercolor crayons are upscale. Crayolas are not, not even in the super big pack with 8,754 colors and the built-in crayon sharpener.
Mommies are upscale if they don't do it all the time. Full-time Mommies are not.

Daddies are upscale if they're never home because they're too busy with their work. Daddies who hang around a lot are not unless they're like Norman Mailer and they work at home.

Lest you think this list if off the mark, take this true story of my friend's two-and-a-half-year-old with the flu. For four fevered days and nights he had scarcely lifted his head from the pillow. His mother had tried to tempt his nonexistent appetite with a variety of goodies—freshly squeezed orange juice, Carr's water biscuits, croissants with a spoonful of Tiptree preserves on them. The small head resting on the pillow had shaken back and forth. No. He didn't want them. He didn't want anything.

On the fifth day he lifted his head from the pillow. His mother leaned close to him. "Sweetheart, do you want something?" she crooned. He nodded. "Something to eat," she implored. He nodded again. At last the child was hungry. Heaven and earth shall be moved that this child will be fed. "What is it, what would you like?" He dropped his head to the pillow. Exhausted, he must think. Long moments pass. His mother waited expectantly. His small head moved upward once more. She waited. He opened his mouth.

"Peking duck," he said.

The defense rests.

What your Stroller Says About you

WHEN Charlie was born, I asked my sister (a veteran of two already) what kind of stroller she had. "Perego," she said. Perego I bought. What I didn't realize was that the birth of my oldest niece had taken place in what amounted to the Stone Age of Baby Strollers and that Perego was merely one of the early examples of stroller evolution. It's like the Cro-Magnon man of strollers. We're into an advanced era here.

Actually you can tell a lot about a Mommy from the stroller she's pushing—from the brand and from what she's got on it, in it, and around it. And this doesn't even include the kid!

Here are a few suggestions you can use to evaluate strollers the next time you should be in the neighborhood of, say, Carl Schurz Park on the first nice Sunday in four months since winter arrived and it's 2 P.M. and the temperature is an unseasonable sixty-five degrees.

1. Maclaren owners—This is a tightly knit clan who firmly believe in the virtues of value, sturdiness, flexibility, and durability. Various striped coverings indicate branches of the clan, such as the red-and-blue

striped family, but with the advent of seat covers and quilted baby bags, these are becoming harder to identify. More prolific Mommies belong here, as this company makes double strollers. *The* stroller of choice some years back, rather like the GM car, but soon to be over taken by (who else?) the Japanese.

2. Aprica owners—These strollers are from the land of the rising sun, and what they say about you is that you're label-conscious and short. Japanese women aren't terribly tall, and this is a stroller best used by midgets. It is, however, the one featured in photos of movie stars (note Jackie Smith pushing her son in an Aprica) and by more than 75 percent of the population of Jewish American Princesses living on the South Shore of Long Island. Its very cumbersomeness when folded also bespeaks royal blood, as no mother in her right mind would go in anything but a taxi with this buggy.

3. Gerry, Perego, etc.—The ho-hum, too-bad, utilitarian brands seem to get the hardest use and serve out their days in a kind of dray-horse dignity all their own. Ben's for Kids on the Upper East Side doesn't even sell Peregos anymore.

As far as accessorizing, note the presence of cutely designed canvas totes neatly affixed to handles (and matching zip-up baby quilt bags). Maclaren and Aprica users also sport a variety of windscreens, sunscreens, rainscreens, and snow guards, while Charlie in his Perego had to be content with a ratty old summer umbrella that dripped gobs of red dye when we got caught in the rain. Noses also turn up at the wrong plastic shopping bags for sandbox toys. Ben's and Eeyore's Books for kids, yes, A & P and those ubiquitous It's a Pleasure to Serve You things, no. Even I, the Rottenest Mommy of All, confess to stashing away my nicer shopping bags for stroller display. It's the very least I can do, considering I bought a Perego.

Charlie and Mommy Among the Yuckies

EVERYONE knows what a Yuppie is. Therefore, it shouldn't take much imagination to figure out that a Baby Yuppie might conceivably be called a Yuckie.

Yuckies are increasing in number by leaps and bounds because their mommies and daddies think it's very "in" to procreate at the age of thirty-five. Yuckies can be identified in the following ways:

1. The sex of Yuckies is never a surprise because over-thirty-five Mommies have amniocentesis and find out the results. Yuppies aren't big on waiting for things. Allowing five months to elapse without knowing the baby's sex when you might have found it out is like applying for Early Decision for college admission and then not opening the envelope.

2. Before a Yuckie is born, he or she is given a shower, which amounts to a deluge (giving rise to the famous saying "Avant moi, le déluge," attributed to Alessandra Sabrina Rothman-Saltzberg). Name merchandise includes Aprica strollers, Snugli carriers, Absorba and Fusen Usagi baby-wear, and Huggies paper diapers. Market analysts are unable to

figure out why Pampers are being bypassed, but believe me, Pampers is truly worried. Right now, Pampers' upscalability is being retooled.

3. By the age of one, a Yuckie must possess the following: a Cabbage Patch doll, a Cabbage Patch preemie, a caregiver (read "babysitter"), a housekeeper (read "maid"), Baby Nikes, monogrammed and embossed personal stationery, his or her first name executed in wooden blocks, handstitched pillows, quilted appliqué on a comforter and/or hanging from a mobile, a computer (and *not* an Apple, either, we're talking IBM here), stock (we're also talking IBM), and a social calendar. Mommies hire caregivers so they don't have to personally shlep the child from gym class to play dates to cooking class to music and dance.

Yuckie play dates are sort of like the dates you had as a kid with the friend who informed you that you weren't allowed to eat in her room or sit on the bed. Their homes are very, very nice, and you and your child may feel just a tad out of water, but your kid plunges right in and totally demolishes the other kid's room. The result? You get to spend precisely five minutes having coffee in Coalport cups and an hour and a half fitting all the pieces back into the Fisher-Price farm, the Sesame Street kitchen, the alphabet letter boards, the large-piece jigsaw puzzles, and the pegboard set. With extra pegs. You then spend another half hour trying to unglue your glassy-eyed child from any one of the twenty toys he wants to take home.

Signs of incipient Yuckiehood to watch out for:

1. A child who pretends he's a Cabbage Patch doll.

2. A child who won't wear anything without a designer name patch.

3. A child who likes the baby-sitter ("caregiver") better than You.

T-Shirts and Bibs Seen in the Windows of Ben's for Kids on the Upper East Side of New York City

I Look Just Like My Mommy
I Look Just Like My Daddy
Born to Spend
Future Doctor
Future Lawyer
Toddler with a future seeks dynamic female.
Must enjoy peanut butter, superheroes, and frogs.
All this and brains, too.
Junior Executive
Born to be Hugged
Future Heartthrob
You've Come a Long Way, Baby
Lord of the Manor
Food Processor

Prenatal Prep

THE word is in—the newest thing now is smart kids. Everyone is supposed to give birth to raving geniuses.

And how, pray tell, are you supposed to accomplish this? You can buy books like *How to Have a Smarter Baby* and videos like "How to Give Your Baby Encyclopedic Knowledge." You teach your offspring things while they're still in utero (unless you feel funny talking to your stomach) and continue to educate them after birth, I guess by finding a time when they're not feeding or sleeping (which gives you about twenty seconds a day when they're newborns, but never mind).

I've got some suggestions for how to help accomplish this based on what I did with Charlie, who's no slouch in the brains department:

1. Educational TV—I let my stomach watch PBS while I was pregnant. If it was something I enjoyed, along the lines of *Masterpiece Theatre*, I watched, too, If it was a nature show or anything I found boring, I read while my stomach watched. Charlie enjoyed *Brideshead Revisited* a great deal but wasn't too keen on *MacNeil-Lehrer* (he takes after his father in this respect). He also loved *Wall Street Week*. His heels went thub-a-dub

at the sound of the ticker tape music that opens the show.

2. Read interesting newspaper stories aloud—Pass on recipes, how to tips, shape up advice, and other great stuff to your fetus. The editorial page bored Charlie, while the prices of co-ops and condos amused him no end. He also loved Ann Landers, from whom you can really learn a great deal.

3. Talk on the phone a lot—Fetuses love to eavesdrop on your private phone conversations. And you know how much encyclopedic knowledge can be transmitted by phone! Charlie learned all the "in" stuff before he got out, simply by listening in on the umbilical cord hookup.

4. Human relations—Don't be afraid to fight in front of the fetus. Fetuses have to learn, just like everyone else, that The Course of True Love Never Runs Smooth, You Always Hurt the One You Love, Love Means Never Having to Say You're Sorry, etc. Fetuses have feelings, too, and when they're born should comprehend the range of emotions represented by a simple "Waaa."

5. Exotic foods—Clue your fetus in to what he's eating. Read him the menu and explain your selections; he might like to know the day's specials, too. I happen to know for a fact that pepperoni pizza, Chicken Cordon Bleu, and Pasta Primavera cross the placenta same as every thing else. Why should his meals be boring just because he's on a liquid diet? Put yourself in his place (go to the bottom of a swimming pool and close your eyes; stay there a good while and try to feel like a fetus. Dull, isn't it?) Wouldn't a little garlic brighten your day?

I'm sure that Charlie is a much brighter, more *interesting* person because of all this prenatal input. Don't be shy! And it never hurts to take your fetus out with you for a stimulating evening of opera, ballet, or even disco dancing. Later in life your efforts will be rewarded with a grown child who might, once in a while, take *you* out, too!

My Baby—a Keepbook for the Eighties

I don't know about you, but I've got my baby book from the Dim Ages Past when I was born. My mother dutifully recorded my birth date, time, weight, length, hospital—then as soon as they got me home stopped making entries. I'm not sure if this is a good sign or a bad one, but it has left me with a 99 percent unused baby book, which, if I'd wanted to, I could have used for Charlie simply by tearing out the first page. This sort of thing doesn't date, does it?

It does. I got a few books when Charlie was born and, because I'm basically compulsive, filled them in. Some of the categories are standard ("Baby's First Syllables") and some outdated ("Baby's First Outing," as if you waited weeks to give the kid some air and then made a hegira out of it), but the overall fix is blah. Why doesn't someone do a more modern version? There could be special features that reflect today's pressing concerns and Mommy's and Daddy's own special angst.

Here's an informal proposal for this guidebook, one that you baby boom parents will find suits your needs a great deal better:

1. A new prebirth section featuring vital facts such as "The Night Baby Was Conceived" (with temperature charts and fertility drugs, a cinch to record), "Baby's First Sonogram" (with a place to paste the Polaroid snap of the fetus), "My Lamaze Class," "Why I Wasn't Able to Have Natural Childbirth" (room to put down *your* version), "Why I'll Never Have Natural Childbirth Again" (for those who did), plus a foldout page to paste in your fetal monitoring strip.

2. Hospital stays are trés short these days, so this section can be jetti soned in favor of, simply, your Obstetrician's Bill. No one is going to believe the price unless you affix a copy here.

3. The going-home section now needs several pages for a list of "Equipment Purchased," single-spaced, in columns please, so as not to run too long. Savvy organizers might appreciate a checklist for name brands (such as diapers or strollers).

4. In addition to gifts received, add a special area for "Baby's First Portfolio." Zero-coupon bonds, stocks, etc., should be dutifully listed, as should brokerage house and "Baby's Financial Advisors" (accountant, lawyer, etc.).

5. Early months must now reflect todays' lifestyle, when Baby now accompanies Mom and Dad everywhere, safely ensconced in a Snugli or carried in a chic wicker basket like a load of wash. Provide room for such events as "Baby's First Four-Star Restaurant," "Baby's First Block buster Movies" ("Slept through *Rambo* but fussed through *Cocoon*"), "Baby's First Power Lunch," "Baby's First Cocktail Party," and, due to additional problems with getting and keeping the right caregiver, "Baby's First, Second, Third, Fourth Nanny/Housekeeper/etc."

6. Because Baby is now so busy at such a young and tender age, leave room for extracurricular activities. Perhaps a page resembling a college class schedule might be inserted, to give Mom and Dad room to note down all the daily events such as gym class, cooking, dance, play dates, visits to the dermatologist, opthalmologist, as well as pediatrician. A section like this, for "Baby's Busy Week," will be much appreciated.

7. Finally, because Baby is now part of the Global Village, some of the following can be included:

"Baby's Favorite MTV Video" (Babies prefer Michael Jackson)
"Baby's Favorite TV Commercial" (most babies like "Milk is a Health Kick!")

"Baby's Favorite Newscaster" (General consensus is Diane Sawyer)
"Baby's Favorite Weekly Magazine" (They love to tear up and/or eat *People*)
"Baby's Favorite Video Cassette" (Babies adore Bing Crosby movies)

    A word of advice: because people seem so concerned with having a baby who is, so to speak, on the cutting edge, a liberal use of such phrases as "state-of-the-art" (as in "state-of-the-art bris") or "custom-designed" (as in "custom-designed potty") will definitely improve sales. I promise.

The Birthday Brigade

SUPPOSE you bought a Fisher-Price mini school bus for your friend's child's birthday, and when she, in turn, handed you your child's present, it was the BIG Fisher-Price School Bus (with twice the number of grinning-idiot plastic children and pets)? Do you crawl under a rock and die, or what??

I can recall an era when it was sufficient to buy a box of crayons and a coloring book, wrap it in Happy Birthday paper, and bring it to a birthday party where all the presents were unwrapped (among them no doubt six other boxes of crayons *and* the same coloring book). However, we are no longer amused by this sort of thing in the Birthday Brigade.

Spiffy parties require even spiffier presents. For tykes under age (say) six, it's tacky to buy clothing unless you're a relative. Mommies quest for toys but decisions are frightening. The Really Important Question rears its ugly, gluttonous head: Does this child already have it? These days, you never know.

I was startled to discover that a Mommy for whom I had purchased a plastic kitchen sink (which works with *real water,* gang) already had it! The height of cool is that she not only didn't say, she kept the second sink. Probably in case the first needed a plumber. But after visiting the child's house and discovering both sinks, I felt like slinking away. I should have known, after all. You're supposed to have Mommy ESP about these things.

It would help, then, if we could compile a list of really *safe* birthday gifts, nonsexist yet sexy, so easy-to-find that even the dumbest of Mommies can master the game. Next time one of those birthday party invitations crosses your mailbox (making you feel as if you'd been subpoenaed) go right to your neighborhood store and buy one of the following:

1. *A real telephone.* Even the five and dime sells phones these days, and kids are tired of their dingy plastic pretend instruments. Throw in a wire and jack, and Mommy and Daddy can easily plug it in the wall when the kid turns five; that seems to be the age at which today's children are getting their own phones. No fads here, please; the staying power of, say, Snoopy, is questionable. A nice Trim-tone model with lighted dial will do.

2. *A real vacuum cleaner.* If your kid, like Charlie, drives you crazy about wanting to use your household appliances, get him one for himself. It's a neat birthday gift, and with a little training a three or four-year-old can do a passable job on a six-room apartment in about three hours (but don't expect him to do windows).

3. *A Salton electric coffee maker.* Charlie's favorite pull-apart and put-together puzzle; an added benefit is, when the child isn't looking, you can make up to thirty cups of coffee for guests.

4. *A set of matched luggage for the Cabbage Patch doll merchandise.* Samsonite or American Tourister will do; when the doll, the doll's sister and premature baby brother are not off to the Bahamas, the family might borrow a few pieces to use. Given the fact that Cabbage Patch dolls now travel with strollers, carriages, carriers, playpens, and the like, you'd better invest in at least a twenty-eight-incher.

When the presents are opened, I guarantee that they won't have a duplicate of yours.

Best Looking, Wittiest, Most Likely to Succeed

TODDLERS have so-o-o-o many things to do to Keep Them Busy. Why, it's just astounding they have any time to play or suck their thumbs or even nap. They are programmed within an inch of their little lives; some Mommies have had to hire Extra Help just to drag the kid from activity to activity.

Which brings me to wonder, what if the next logical step were a *Nursery School Yearbook*, presented to the graduating class, listing all of their extracurricular activities? It would read something like this:

Kimberley Amanda Evergreen—"I Want a Girl Just Like the Girl Who Married Dear Old Dad"; Tumbling and Baby Gymnastics 1 and 2; Gourmet Cooking 2 and 3; Rhythm and Dance Dynamics 2, 3, and 4; Build Your Own Puppet Theater 4; Creative Writing 5.

Jonathan Livingston Katz—"Still Waters Run Deep"; Gymboree 2, 3, and 4; International Relations 2 and 3; Songwriting and Guitar 4; Psychotherapy 3, 4, and 5.

Sophie Kelly—"I Wish They All Could Be California Girls"; transferred from Beverly Hills, Ca. Surfing 3; Sufi 3 and 4; Tofu 1, 2, and 3.

Farfetched? How about the New Jersey nursery school with graduates arrayed in pastel mortar- boards and gowns, marching in to the strains of Pomp and You-Know-What?

Or the Scarsdale Mom who, afraid her small daughter wasn't faring well in her gymnastics class, hired a tutor?

I think I'm going to run right out and enroll Charlie in Dalcroze Eurythmics.

Item from our Catalogue

A plastic barbecue grill, around two-and-a-half-feet high, with a lid that lifts, on four wheels so it can be moved from place to place. Beneath the grill is a realistic photo of glowing coals that is exposed at the flick of a switch to On. Three pieces of meat are included, raw on one side, charred on the other, and several chef's tools. The tot places the seared side *down*, raw side up, and "cooks" the meat, then flips it over onto its raw side to expose the cooked part. Apron and chef's hat *not* included.

*A jug of Wine,
a Loaf of Bread, and
a Three-Year-Old
Singing in the
Wilderness*

"I'll Just Pick"

As even *The New York Times* reports, grazing is a national pastime, the eating style of choice these days. Restaurants of the moment sponsor grazing menus on which the largest portions of food turn out to be the bread and butter. You eat minipizzas, microportions of pasta, itty-bitty salads, and teeny desserts with mellifluous names like tiramisu. (One wonders if the *next* generation of kids might not be given names after their parents' favorite foods: Tiramisu Bernstein, Pagliaefieno O'Brien, Carpaccio Peabody III—you get the idea.)

Of course *everyone* wants to take credit for identifying or inventing food fads, but I've got a corner here on the food scene to nominate for the Earl of Sandwich award. In recognition of his contribution to the art of dining in the eighties, in grateful appreciation, the Grazing Award goes to *Charlie*. Let's have a big hand, folks!

Charlie has been grazing ever since he could ingest solids (and I don't mean pennies and stepped-on chewing gum from the sidewalk, either). Adults have always looked to the Very Young for their fads and trends, and they were quick to pick this up from my son.

Let me explain how this works and how Charlie has become a veritable Amerigo Vespucci of food explorers.

First of all, Charlie never eats anything on *his* plate. This is one of the most noticeable trends among grazers: they continually taste each other's foods. In restaurants, they must do this because they are served so little food they have to supplement elsewhere. Charlie does it because his favorite activity is to make you cook something special just for him ("Hot cereal, I want hot cereal!") and then after it's all ready and you're waiting expectantly, he won't touch a bite. Isn't that fun, Mommies and Daddies? Naturally you can really work up an appetite torturing your mother and father this way, so you collect your calories from *their* plates.

Another hallmark of grazing is eating bits and pieces of things unrelated to each other, a kind of wild tasting spree. Charlie has done that for years. He thinks nothing of having pickle and applesauce (thank goodness I don't have to worry about him being pregnant!). He'll have a bite of your salad with blue cheese dressing and then consume a mouthful of his own french toast with half a bottle of Aunt Jemima syrup poured on it. Take that, Paul Prudhomme!

Due to the vagaries of Big City life-styles, grazers also eat at very odd hours. First of all, there's that interminable wait at the bar for the Right Table. Then there's the s-l-o-w service accorded you by your hip, chic, inexperienced but lavishly charming waiter or waitress. Then there's the need to cook totally from scratch, observed by all diners in your immaculate open-to-view kitchen. Next thing they'll have you watch them killing lobsters and plucking chickens (free-range, of course). Well, take a leaf from my kid's book; he was there *first!* Eat at regular mealtimes? Phooey! Eat at least one of each of the seven basic food groups in any recognizable order? Double phooey!

Here is what Charlie, in one typical day, eats, and the time at which he eats it:

8:30 A.M. One mouthful of Rice Krispies and milk because his father has threatened him with no *Mr. Rogers' Neighborhood* until he's twenty-three. A glass of apple juice.

9:30 A.M. One-quarter of a piece of toast with Velveeta while watching *Sesame Street.* Half the cheese ends up smeared on the TV screen as Charlie greets his favorite segments by embracing the tube. A glass of apple juice.

11 A.M. Half of a 25¢ bag of sour cream and onion potato chips in the supermarket as a bribe so Mommy won't be ejected from the store because of various carryings-on.

Noon An index finger of yolk from a fried egg. Another glass of apple juice.

3 P.M. One-quarter of half a bagel smeared with cream cheese. More apple juice.

4:30 P.M. One soft chocolate chip cookie (along with cookie Charlie sings chorus of "Crispy, Chewy" commercial; it's like putting a coin in a jukebox. He won't eat the cookie without playing the tune). Apple juice encore.

6:30 P.M. Four bites of lettuce and Wishbone Italian dressing (a.k.a. sauce), two bites of chicken off a drumstick, the tops off a piece of broccoli (a.k.a. trees). All of this is off your plate, so then you have to finish up his portion, which has been cut into minuscule pieces and is now all mashed together.

8 P.M. Some of your evening snack of ice cream and probably the whole dish if you'd let him.

Chinese Bones

WHETHER it's takeout, ordering in, or carryout, a meal procured by picking up the phone by any other name is dinner in our house. Who's got time to cook these days, and besides, how can you feel guilty about something that *Time* and *Newsweek* and Rupert Murdoch and Co. have all agreed is the chic thing to do. Ordering out is in.

It's usually Chinese over here, and Charlie has been bred to like the stuff. He particularly favors what he calls Chinese bones, his term for spare-ribs. But more than the eating, he likes the ordering. You know those plastic kid phones all the toddlers have? He uses his to pretend he's calling in an order. Then he hangs up his phone, waits, and says, "ding-dong." That's the guy coming to our door.

Chinese people love children, and the food deliverers are charmed by my son, who appears at our front door in various stages of undress to say, "Hi, Chinese man. You got food for us? I want to give you money. Thank you." The men smile indulgently, and Charlie politely wishes them well. Lately he's taken to asking if the ring of the front doorbell doesn't mean Chinese bones at odd hours, such as 11 A.M., when it's actually the exterminator.

One night, a bit tired of chicken with black bean sauce, etc., we decided to call a sushi bar that had opened up nearby and promised free delivery. We phoned in our order, and Charlie hopped around, chattering about his Chinese bones and Chinese soup. "No," I corrected. "We're having Japanese food tonight."

"Japanese," he tried as if tasting the new word as he said it.

When the doorbell rang, I was in the kitchen. Charlie and his Daddy answered the door, and I could hear Charlie chatting away. "Hi, Japanese man. You bring the food? You a Japanese man?"

After the door closed, the two came into the kitchen. "That was nice," I said to my husband. "Isn't it smart how Charlie remembered it was a Japanese man and all? So cute!"

"There was only one problem," my husband said. "The guy delivering the food was black."

Eat to Win

In the old days you fed toddlers Toddler Food. After they got their teeth and stopped gumming the stuff out of jars, they were switched to regular food carefully cooked and monitored. A perfect little baby lamb chop, for example, mashed potatoes whipped to a fare-thee-well, tiny little baby canned peas artfully arranged in a three-part dish that plugged into the wall and had, ironically, painted lambs frisking on the bottom beneath the food.

If you think that I stand around at lunchtime making itsy-bitsy lamb chops, you're out of your mind. But while I'm in a confessing mood, I'm going to make a list of some of Charlie's favorite foods just to indicate how much times (and Mommies) have changed. All of that "He-really-shouldn't-be-eating-something-so-rich-or-spicy-or-whatever" has gone out the window.

Charlie loves

Blue cheese salad dressing
Sour pickles
Grated Parmesan cheese licked off his index finger
Raw egg (but not cooked)

Nachos and bean dip
White wine spritzers
Garlic bread
Hot dogs you buy from the cart in the street
Peanut butter ice cream bars with caramel and chocolate topping
Doritos
Root beer
Dijon mustard
Velveeta and bologna sandwiches
Nova Scotia salmon
Lentil soup

Please do not send me any mail on the subject of Charlie's eating habits, as I shall return these envelopes marked Addressee Unknown. I know I may have set the baby lamb chop industry back a few light years, but perhaps I can give hope to those mothers who have given birth to what were once called picky eaters. Yesterday's picky eater is tomorrow's galloping gourmet.

It's Only your Entire Future Hanging in the Balance

(Nursery School in the Year Two)

Charlie (and Mommy) go to Nursery School

MAYBE it's my imagination, but I think I actually miss my two-year-old son while he's at nursery school more than he misses me. Of course we experienced separation anxiety at the beginning. I left; he screamed. I was secretly pleased. After all, if he didn't scream, what did that say about me?

But now the teachers tell me proudly he doesn't ask where Mommy is. He kisses me good-bye at the door and walks calmly away. He is doing "very well." But is Mommy doing well?

> He doesn't miss me.
> He gets along fine without me.
> He won't tell me what he does during that mysterious three hours we are apart. It is his secret from me.
> "How was school," I ask.
> "Ummmmmm, hummmmm," he says.
> "Did you have a nice snack?"
> "Snack," he repeats.
> "What did you have?" I press on.
> "Apple juice," he answers. And that is the only thing he *ever* says about snack.
> "Do you have some nice friends?" Mommy inquires politely.

"Friends," he says.

It is painfully obvious to me that except for the little I can glean from the teachers and the other mothers, Charlie's nursery school experience belongs to him alone. Entirely alone. And that Mommy, seated expectantly outside the closed door, is *out*.

I'll just have to think of this as good preparation for when he goes to college.

Charlie and Mommy Continue to go to Nursery School...

THE mysteries of my son's three-hour twice weekly mornings continue to unfold. I am being initiated into the secrets of his separate existence v-e-r-y s-l-o-w-l-y.

He comes home from school a silent, tiny Buddha, clutching superior foodstuffs in his hand. He does not offer Mommy a bite. "Did you make this?" No reply. The muffins, pancakes, cookies, etc., look delicious.

He sings strange songs that I have not taught him. One day it's "Wind, Wind, Wind the Bobbin." The next week it's something that sounds like "Wrinkle Bells." I cannot ascertain if this is, indeed, Jingle, or some other familiar bells. The tune goes elsewhere.

He even contributes to Thanksgiving, with a small glass-jarred gift of what he calls honey. I explain that this is cranberry sauce to eat with the turkey. He sticks to his notion of honey and wants desperately to eat it on the end of his finger. When Thanksgiving comes and we serve it, properly, on his plate, he won't touch it.

And he makes things in school. It's hard to feel like a proper parent, even after spending nights walking the floor with a crying child or throwing a birthday party complete with Cookie Monster on the cake, until that Magical Moment when someone hands you a picture with your kid's name on it.

Of course, then Competitive Momhood 101 takes over, and you Compare. "Well, everybody else's has the pieces lined up so neatly and the girls seem to be more artistic and nobody else uses four gobs of paste on one little shred of construction paper." Mommy wants to know why it's not Up There on the Wall, next to the Others.

Is this what nursery school is like for everyone, I wonder? It's hard to say, because if you get together with other Mommies, what you talk about most is . . . getting into private school.

Mommy goes to Charlie's Teacher Conference

THE schedule for teacher conferences goes up on the bulletin board. I go home in a cold sweat. "What's your problem?" says my husband. "They don't give out grades."

Ha. They may not give out report cards, but this is worse. They're going to tell me how my son is faring as a Human Being. Isn't nursery school Real Life in Microcosm? It isn't exactly school, no homework or alphabet or phys ed. So what they'll tell me about Charlie is whether he is *good*.

The night before I don't sleep. I sit up and practice reading upside down and backward.

Next day I am there promptly. I wear makeup. I have put in my contact lenses. Maybe they won't remember that slob with the thick glasses and green complexion who always picks the kid up.

Wendy Sue is sweet and nice. She puts a Written Report on My Son smack on the desk between us. I squint and try to use my newly acquired reading skills.

She tells me he's getting along fine. He is very good at some activities.

"Like what?" I ask, realizing I still don't know exactly what it is they're doing all morning. Will they tell me how good he is at snack, for example? Well-adjusted at apple juice, I guess, but not so good at hard cheese.

"Stringing beads," I am told. Charlie is very good. Good hand-eye coordination. Oh, I'm starting to see this is real. They notice like crazy how he is getting along. I start to sweat again.

"Uh, um, er, do any of the, er, other children do this, um, activity well?" I ask, angling for that basis of comparison we all need so we can apply to Hunter primary, get them in, don't pass Go, and collect eight thousand dollars a year not spent on private school.

"Oh, all the children do well at things. One of the boys is terrific at puzzles, really does them well, while another child is fantastic at building things." Wendy Sue is truly a Kissinger when it comes to conferences. I am stymied.

I am finally able to decipher one of the upside-down words at long last. Is it the secret to Charlie's hidden I.Q. potential? His future at M.I.T.? What does the word say? It says "Lotto."

I am too embarrassed to ask if the kids have won any money yet.

Charlie goes to Harvard (Someday)

IT'S even made *The New York Times*—can you believe it? Nursery school Mommies and their anxiety about getting the kids into the Right School and teaching them the Right Stuff. I'm ashamed to confess I've had impure thoughts about the future, but I counter them with the realities of the present. Charlie's getting prepped already. It's there in the curriculum for all to see. What you need is the correct mind-set and an attitude we shall call, for lack of a better term, Baby Boomish.

Charlie's nursery school day starts with *arrival and greeting*. When Charlie's a big hot-shot doctor or lawyer and he's arrived, he'll be greeted each day in similar fashion. Now this is the way to start!

The *gross motor activity* that follows is a head start on all the right moves he'll need to excel at lacrosse, racquetball, squash, tennis, and all those other lovely Ivy League type activities. Later on, when he plays golf at his Club, he'll be extra glad he got his start early.

Meeting in the circle? What could be a more natural introduction to seminars and, later, board meetings? Learning to sit and listen to others is a greatly needed talent.

Of course Charlie needs the refueling of *snack* to continue his arduous day; the healthful foods served will keep him in fighting trim for our dog-eat-dog world.

Washing his cup is a fabulous learning experience, as executives, doctors, and lawyers must all realize that this is a man's and a woman's world. No sexism in the nursery school! This will surely help Charlie to become a well-adjusted, nonchauvinistic leader of people.

Rest and story time let those old alpha waves just flow. Attitudes encouraging biofeedback and getting in touch with the body must be a part of a hectic, upwardly mobile life-style if we are not to raise a pack of Type As who'll conk out early!

With *free play*, Charlie learns to retool his skills for the crunch that lies ahead. Negotiating over the water table, making deals with cars and trucks, dissecting the innards of a puzzle, all of these talents will help Charlie move into proper post position for future achievements.

So there you have it, parents. Why waste another moment worrying about SAT scores and I.Q. tests? Start your planning *now*. Don't allow your child to be Left Behind. Every day, in nursery schools throughout the land, toddlers are gaining on other toddlers. Remember, Harvard is watching *You*.

Status Snacks

As anxious parents send their offspring to nursery schools at younger and younger ages, the quest for the Status Snack begins earlier, too. Many schools sponsor cooperative snack programs for the toddlers, in which parents themselves supply the daily fare. In a class averaging around twelve children, you might be called upon to furnish provisions three to four times per year.

Advice must be given. Snackoreconomics is a vital part of supply-demand in early childhood education. Kids demand food; parents (on schools' insistence) supply. Competition surges among Concerned Mommies. Here's a quick lesson in How to Properly Ensnack Your Child's Nursery School Class (Plus Teachers).

1. Be Creative—Remember that these are jaded palates; you want to get Bonbel miniature Baby Gouda cheeses in the little net bag, each individually wrapped in its own wax cover? Forget it. These children have been Bonbeled from Birth. A nice goat cheese from Zabar's might do the trick; Carr's water biscuits are the proper accompaniment. A few green grapes to follow, and voila, you've done your turn.

2. Don't be Tacky—If you go the cheap route, *everyone* will know. You cannot cut up a half brick of Velveeta and disguise it by sticking in frilly toothpicks. Besides, Ralph Nader frowns on frilly toothpicks for children under age five. Kraft French Dressing removed from its tell tate bottle and dumped into a Pyrex dish will not do as a dip for crudités either. These are the Cuisinart Kids; fresh green mayonnaise might do, but only if your cut-up veggies go Beyond Celery and Carrots. Try snow peas and baby zucchini, so conveniently sized for small mouths, too.

3. Sugar is a No-No—The quickest way to earn the collective wrath of the Mommies is to provide Sugar Treats for Their Child. You run the risk of a lawsuit, for heaven's sake. A good rule of thumb is to treat each kid like a virgin. A granule of sugar may never have passed these lips before, so why run the risk of all that guilt. Sugar substitutes are even worse (don't ask what they've linked to cyclamates and NutraSweet). Saccharin could get you tossed out of nursery school on your ear! The days of good old milk and cookies went out with x-raying feet in shoe stores. Even teething infants aren't gnawing on zwieback these days. It's more like Ka-Me sesame crackers they drool over; never mind that they look like craters on the moon and smell like frozen shrimp.

4. You Can Fool Some of the People Some of the Time, but You Can't Fool Mom—And if you should believe, foolishly, that the kids won't remember what they ate anyway and no one really cares, Think Again. Charlie knows pasteurized process cheese at twenty paces. And I know at least a half-a-dozen Mommies who say they can tell if their kid has had sugar by what dance routines they perform an hour after eating. So if your kid does a version of "Beat It" in your living room an hour after nursery school, no doubt some Rotten Mommy has slipped him an Oreo.

Typhoid Mommy

I'M not a big one on keeping children home from school. If they're sick, yes, of course. Fever, a bad cold, stomach virus. Cruel I'm not. I remember as a child seeing doctors' kids (it was always doctors' kids, wasn't it?) come to school with horrible head colds and tissues stuffed up their sweater sleeves. One child had to have *at least* 102° in order to be allowed the privilege of Staying Home From School Sick. My mother's liberal rule was twenty-four hours at home, without temperature, following any illness. Neat, huh?

Which brings me to poor Charlie, whose Mommy sneaks in to the typewriter and works when he's not here, so she's kind of Rotten in this department. Yes, I confess that he's had some fever one day and none the next AND I LET HIM GO BACK TO NURSERY SCHOOL WITHOUT WAITING TWENTY-FOUR HOURS. Bad Mommy.

Recently I did something even worse. In spite of the fact that Charlie had a teeny weeny temperature, maybe 99.3° or so, and some little spots on his hands and feet (red-and-white) I let him go to school. Now this might have been chicken pox, scourge of the nursery school, and one does *not* send one's child to school with possible C.P. But since the blotches had faded and didn't itch and no new ones appeared and whoever heard of chicken pox only on the hands and feet and my husband thinks I'm a total flake on the subject of germs anyway (he's pre-Pasteur in his attitudes), I sent Charlie on his way. I then discovered, via a chat with my pediatrician, that I had probably exposed an entire group of kids to what is called (I kid you not) Coxsackie Virus.

A.k.a. hand, foot, and mouth disease.

A.k.a. Total Embarrassment.

You get no brownie points with Coxsackie Virus. At least with chicken pox everyone is interested. "When did he come down with it?" "What was the incubation period?" "Is it a mild case or a bad one?" Mommies huddle in groups, counting backward on their fingers to see if *their* child was exposed. And of course there's a medal-of-honor aspect to chicken pox, too. You get it, you get over it, you're done. "Phew, at least I'm finished with *that* for the rest of my life!"

Coxsackie Virus is not a Status Illness.

Who cares if you get Coxsackie Virus? Who's ever even *heard* of Coxsackie Virus? I'll bet the people who live in Coxsackie don't even know they've got a disease named after their town!

The Mommies think you're making it up. They call to see What's Wrong and you tell them, "Coxsackie Virus."

"*What* does he have?" chorus the Mommies, sup- pressing their mirth at the very notion that a child of theirs could catch something with such a ridiculous name.

You quote the pediatrician. They ask you if it's in Spock. You tell them it's not (another strike against it).

And worst of all, you have to keep the kid away from other kids because Coxsackie Virus is *catching*. So now we're exiled from the park, the school, etc., because of this idiotic Thing with the Silly Name.

On further thought, if they were going to name it after a city, couldn't they have called it something like Acapulco Disease or Cap d'Antibes Fever?

Charlie and Mommy get Promoted

As the end of the first year of nursery school approaches, Mommies reflect on their experience. Many wonder, "How has my child changed? What has my child learned?" Conversely, the Mommies wonder, "What have *I* learned?"

I wonder, too. It's pretty obvious to me what Charlie has learned. I could make a list:

1. *Cleanup*—Before attending nursery school, Charlie would sit and watch while Mommy cleaned up the mess in his room, sorting out Fisher-Price families and other delicate operations. But now Charlie has learned a special song in school. And when we have cleanup at home, Charlie sings, "Cleanup, Cleanup, one-two-three," while he sits and watches Mommy cleaning up the mess in his room.

2. *Sharing*—One of the principal reasons you send your child to nursery school is so he can Socially Interact like a mensch. Before his school experience, Charlie would grab toys away from other children when he wanted what they had. Now he vociferously exclaims, "Share!" as

he grabs toys away from other children.
3. *Widened Horizons*—Charlie has been introduced to a remarkable spetrum of new concepts and ideas and has, in fact, embraced all of them wholeheartedly. Some of the cultural interchange he has imported to our house includes Mr. T, correct lexicography (yesterday he politely but firmly informed me that it was a "banister" and not a "rail"), marriage (he calls the spouse of one of his teachers "Husband," as in "Hi, Husband, how you?"), nonviolence (when he saw me playfully slapping his father's thigh, he announced, "No hitting, no biting!"), and those things he calls "Caah-Patch" dolls.

And Mommy's Widened Horizons?

Well, my graduation speech will be selected from one of the followed Pertinent Topics:

1. How to Talk on the Phone Without Saying, "OHMYGOD HOLDONAMINUTE!"
"He usually screams like that."
"He'll be fourteen in eleven years and two months."

2. How to Browse (pronounced brouz, as in perambulating around a place of business such as a boutique and taking more than five seconds to examine a piece of merchandise; can be applied to trips to a department store such as Bloomingdale's, if you can remember where that is, as long as your trip does not exceed the length of time it takes you to get back by noon to pick up the kid).

3. Walking Out of the Supermarket Without Purchasing: Cheez Doodles, Gum, Pepperidge Farm Sugar Cookies, Granny Smith Apples with One Bite Taken Out of Them, and Some Kind of Totally Awful Gray Hair Tint Your Kid Shoplifted but You Were Too Embarrassed to Say So and You Bought It for $8.99.

Mommy and Charlie, go to the head of the class!

The Toddler Network

My Dentist is my Best Friend

REMEMBER dentists? They wore nasty-looking white coats buttoned on one shoulder. They had grim offices decorated with tatty magazines and smelling of antiseptic. They were old and inured to the screams of children. And they most certainly did not (like pediatricians in those days) give out lollipops.

Them times has changed, and upscale Mommies wouldn't dream of such atrocities for their children. To begin, you don't wait until your kid screams in the night with toothache agony to visit the dentist; up-to-the-moment Moms start the checkups around the age of three. This means we enter the realm of Toddler Dentistry, and with it comes Your Friend Who Also Happens to Be Your Dentist.

Charlie loves his dentist. The dentist inhabits an office with a separate toy and play area stocked with blocks and a garage for cars and dolls and trucks and books of all kinds. And these are not tacky old toys like the ones at the pede's, these are of a reasonably new vintage. The office is cheery and painted in bright colors with dozens of Polaroids of smiling, happy, white-toothed satisfied tots affixed to the walls. There's not a white coat to be seen. Charlie's dentist wears crew-necked sweaters and runs in the New

York City Marathon. He looks like a college kid. He, too, smiles a lot and, for nervous Moms, carries a beeper for twenty-four hour on-call service. And this is for teeth!

On entering the office, which is a long, open space with no claustrophobic cubicles, Charlie is shown a nice dental video filled with smiling mouths, straight teeth, and giddy toothbrushes pushing for good care. Charlie watches videos; Mommy reads dental degrees on the wall (plus marathon certificates). Exams take place in the sunshine from floor-to-ceiling windows; Charlie wears Mickey Mouse sunglasses and gets to see himself in his own dazzling hand mirror. Kindly Smurfs with dental equipment perch on a nearby ledge. Everything is so low-key it's less traumatic than a visit to the shoe store. No anxiety. No fears. No pain. And surely this *isn't* a dentist, the crewnecked sweaters say.

Charlie gets to pick from the toy jar (slimy plastic worms and spiders, rubber finger puppets, and wheelless cars), while Mommy is reassuringly reassured. Mommy is falling in love, too. And to think they even do orthodontia. I'm ready to sign up for life. And can my husband come here, too, I'm wondering?

A month after our visit we get a card in the mail, addressed to Charlie. It has a cute cartoon on one side and a message on the other. "Glad your teeth are well. Looking forward to seeing you again. Your friend." It's signed by his dentist.

In England they make knights out of such people.

Chatting Up the Caregiver

THE problem, to be specific, is play dates. Everyone remembers play dates when they themselves were tykes. Your Mommy arranged with another Mommy for you to visit their house or to come to your place; when children were very young the Mommies came along. Then you played Decapitate the Barbie Doll while the Mommies sat at the kitchen table with Dugan's cupcakes and mugs of instant coffee, telling nasty stories about the president of the PTA and somebody's doctor-husband.

Times have changed, for Mommies have returned to work, and the caregivers have taken over. Make a date with a Mommy? I'm the Mommy; the other kids have hired help. You want a social life with your kid, you're going to have to learn to chat up the caregivers.

There are several kinds of caregivers (baby-sitters, housekeepers, nannies, and the lot) who may turn up at your front door. The first is black, possibly West Indian, kind, gentle, delightful with the children, a wonderful person. What do you say when they bring the child to your house to play? "I had a lovely vacation last year visiting your native island"? "It's more than a beach, it's a country"?

If the caregiver is from abroad, you may run into a different set of problems; she may not speak English. I know no German or Spanish (save for Achtung! and Olé!) and must mime certain niceties like, "Would you like sugar in your coffee?" If they do speak a bit of English, you can while away the afternoon discussing immigration problems ("Do you plan to get a Green Card?" is a good opener).

Then there are the grandmotherly, older types who come in and Take Over. They've been at this for a million years; they issue loads of instructions and tell you what you're doing wrong, making you feel like an even more incompetent Mommy than you already do. Theirs are the children to whom you must *never* offer cookies. "You really should throw that nasty thing away," is how they preface all their instructions, the thing being a balloon on a string, a bag of Oreos, anything that comes to a point including kitchen equipment and your husband, or imitation kid versions of the real thing, toy thermometers, plastic food, etc. All of this is conveyed with enormous Fear and Trembling, and you, superstitious and by now terrified, instantly obey. You come to understand that this caregiver runs the other household with an iron hand and, given enough time, will run yours. Many of these women were formerly baby nurses (the kind who never let you near your own baby even if you were breast-feeding).

As the day progresses, I find myself dredging up odd bits of information about myself, things I never realized before, like: "It's very stimulating to spend a day with a two-year-old, isn't it?" Or "I find myself actually watching *Romper Room* for the content, don't you?" This can make for a very interesting afternoon. One caregiver showed me how she does cornrows.

There's no real solution to this Culture Gap, save for the obvious one: hire your own caregiver, present her with the phone list, and let the caregivers have their own play dates. God knows how this will work out, but at least you won't have to Make Chat.

Sundays, Mondays, Tuesdays, Wednesdays, Thursdays, Fridays, and Saturdays in the Park with George, Marissa, Alessandra, Evan, Courtenay, and Jason

YOU know these Mommies. They're the Park Mothers. They arrive early in the morning, unpack their provisions from the strollers as if they were unloading the mules, and set up camp.

They are going to stay in the park All Day. They are doing this because the park is their backyard and their children need Fresh Air and Sunlight and Other Kids. Mainly, however, it's the Mommies who need relief.

And how do you spell relief? G-E-T O-U-T O-F T-H-E H-O-U-S-E.

What does one need to set up shop on a park bench for, say, around eight hours? Depending on the child's age, a remarkable range of equipage must be hauled over, dangling from the stroller handles, bursting out of tote bags, jammed into plastic shopping bags, and ensconced on the child's own lap. The average Park Tot (aged two to three) needs most of the following:

1. Extra diapers (generally the prince or princess is not trained early).

2. Premoistened wipes (for tushy and for food accidents as well, also handy for the occasional bloody nose or knee).

3. Small plastic bag for used diapers; only the unfastidious throw them raw into trash barrels.

4. Extra set of clothes because you never know.

5. Box of unsweetened, unsalted snack: pretzels (from the health food store, spinach flour base), potato chips (from the health food store, soy flour base), crackers (from the health food store, rice flour base), nuts (from the health food store, usually sunflower seeds).

6. Bag of sweet snack, all-natural sugar only (though honey may be permissible): mock chocolate (from the health food store, carob base), cookies (from the health food store, oatmeal base), candies (from the health food store, sesame and honey), raisins (from the health food store, though they're probably the same as the ones sold at the A & P).

7. The Juice of Choice: Red Cheek Apple Juice, natural style.

8. Lunch: natural peanut butter (the kind that separates into a puddle of oil on top and the good stuff on the bottom), wheat-germ bread, carrot sticks, cheese cubes, bran muffins, apple slices (peeled), wedges of orange (unpeeled). Your lunch? You buy the crummy hot dog from the man with the cart and wolf it down when Junior isn't looking.

9. A riding toy: the late, lamented Marx CHIPS motorcycle used to be all the rage (and still fetches a handsome price *used*), but riding toys have a way of disappearing just like their namesake TV shows; Knight Rider is now popular, and Hello, Kitty seems to be holding its own. Riding toys are not, however, ridden *to* the park, because if the prince or princess tires after eight hours, *you'll* have to ride it home. Two-wheeled

toys are slung over the handles of the stroller and pushed to the park along with everything else by Mommy-Coolie. When your toddler demands to ride the toy himself and tells you to leave the stroller home, DON'T GIVE IN. INSIST. YOU'LL BE SORRY IF YOU DON'T.

10. Sand toys: these are the great bone(s) of contention in park circles, so label with magic marker or Property of . . . stickers. (There's a sticker/lag in such labels of about ten years between fashionable and unfashionable names. Go and find Amber, Ashley, or Brett, for example. Uh-uh. but there are dozens of out-of-style labels to be had, Nancy, Linda, Barbara and the like. I never have a problem finding Charlie, for instance, while Mommies of all those Jareds are out of luck.) Pails and shovels aren't so popular anymore, except for chic little painted metal pails like you had as a kid that used to cost $.50 and now go for $3.79. Shovels should be bloated into oversized shapes on long handles and accompanied by matched gardening tools: hoe, rake, etc. The most coveted sand toys are the trucks; a junior World Trade Center could be erected with all the bulldozers, sand haulers, rollers, steam shovels, etc., that vroom all day long. And just when you thought you'd licked the envy problem by purchasing the $39.99 superdeluxe, rotary-action, Killer-Death, Subtransformer, Turbo-Engine Digging Machine, your kid screams bloody murder because some little girl in the sandbox won't give up her Tupperware lid.

11. A sweater or jacket in case it gets cold (for the kid, not for you).

12. Reading matter: if you think you're going to have time to read, you're out of your mind. But certain status publications bespeak a commitment to Motherhood— *Parents Magazine* (not *Cosmo*), better still a two-month-old copy of *The New York Times Magazine* section ("I'm sooooo busy I simply haven't had time to even *glance at* the paper!").

Once in the park, you stay. No one wants to be the first to leave. Mommies who do had better have a Good Excuse: "Sorry, I've got to go. Trisha has an appointment with the opthalmologist. I don't think she blinks frequently enough." Other Good Excuses include: going into labor, private school interviews, going to the emergency room for stitches on a just-inflicted park wound, and moving to the suburbs. Regular pediatrician visits are not a good excuse because True Park Mommies make doctor appointments only on rainy days (How do *they* know? They just do).

Park Mommies know each other by their kids. You are recognized as

"Charlie's Mommy" or the-mother-of-the-kid-who . . . The latter is a kind of purgatory, as Mommies are tolerant of aberrant behavior as long as it isn't chronic. Your kid acts like a creep and he's got one more chance. After that, you and he get pegged. Nonviolence scores big with Park Mommies, as no one wants to raise a Future Terrorist.

As to the daily schedule, all you need to do is spend eight hours or so in any park observing. (Author's note: Ha! I dare you!) But after a while a pattern does emerge, a kind of ebb and flow of Mommies and their young, an urban barnyard. While the kids "play," the Mommies discuss comfortable footwear (Mommies in high heels are suspect) and how many sand toys they've lost in the past month. Current records indicate a claim for eleven pails, nine shovels, two trucks, and a three-carat diamond engagement ring (not a sand toy, but it certainly adds a certain je ne sais quoi to the *Guinness Book* entry).

Where are the caregivers in all this? Oh, they're around, but this is the last Flourishing Civilization of Full-Time Mothers, the last holdouts. The Mommies watch the caregivers, forming opinions on which ones are Good and which ought to be fired (though they don't tell the Working Moms, who have a tendency to make Park Moms feel like drudges, drones, and throwbacks). Park Moms are also coolly aloof from other Mommies who aren't regulars.

How, then, does this culture flourish when so many trends encroach on its well-being?

I don't know. I, for one, was under the impression that everyone in New York City had a sitter from the West Indies and that a generation of toddlers was going to grow up saying things like, "Hey, mon, how you like that reggae?" Surprise, surprise, I discovered after Charlie. Mommies are alive and well and institutionalized in the park. (Though like Holden Caulfield and the ducks in *The Catcher in the Rye*, I do wonder where they go in the dead of winter.)

But don't worry if you can't crack the sorority. There's always the Ninety-second Street Y, where, for a cool two hundred bucks or so, you can pay for the privilege of sitting in a room with other Mommies and watching your children "interact" (for all that money you don't think they're simply gong to "play," do you?) at something called, appropriately, "Parkbench." It's extremely popular and is given on weekends and evenings as well, to accommodate Working Mommies and Daddies, lest no one miss out on the singular joys of Park Motherhood.

Contents of Typical Stroller Bag

One box of premoistened wipes, cheap pop up kind semi dried-up from being in there so long
One by now yucky paper diaper "in case"
A half-eaten apple, quite brown
Sticky pull-tabs from top of mini apple juice cans
Three bent straws (used)
Gum wrappers
Extra paper napkins from ice cream truck
One red robot-car transformer toy
Small plastic bag of stale oatmeal cookies, which kid never liked anyway and which are now pulverized
Two mail-order catalogues specializing in items to organize your household
A broken pinwheel
Paper wrapping from guilt gift purchased at

stationery store after slugging tantruming
child (cardboard wrapping, plastic
cover, and brown bag)
Chewed chewing gum, no wrapping
Ends of unfinished hot dog roll
Valium

Do you Consider a Box of Pampers Carry-on Luggage?

The Wings of Boy

CHARLIE Flies! is a little like Garbo Talks! Hugely anticipated but not at all what it was cracked up to be. Why not? I guess I could blame it on the airlines forgetting to fill our order for his Superduper Kid's Extraspecial lunch complete with hot dog, chips, ice cream, cookies, and enough junk food to win them a citation from Vicky Lansky . . . but I won't.

The first time Charlie Flew (last year) we sat in the center section of the plane. Small Charlie, perched on his father's lap, had no idea what was up. We had gotten into this conveyance down a long tunnel, and as we started into motion we rolled forward. Charlie said, "We're on a bus." Yeah, sure, kid. Greyhound. No hassles, no tears, no sweat.

This year? Charlie is hip. He knows we're at an airport. "It's an airport," he says as we pull up to the terminal. Chattering brightly, he points out everything he's seen in miniature in his Richard Scarry books: baggage carts, jets, helicopters, fuel trucks, etc. Mommy and Daddy exchange proud glances. See? we say to each other. He's *prepared*.

But are *we* prepared? We should have told him it was a bus. "And those wings that stick out make the bus go faster, and look, here's the *pilot* of the bus . . ."

This year Charlie required his own seat, which meant his own seat belt and no Daddy's or Mommy's lap, which meant that when we got on the plane and put him in said seat—instant catatonia. The chatterbox of only a few minutes before was reduced to . . . the Mummy.

"Charlie, look, isn't this nice? You're right next to a window!"

His thumb is in his mouth. Not a great sign. He wants Bankie. I glance at Daddy. This is going to be grim.

I open his favorite picture book. Charlie's eyes are fixed, pupils dilating. He isn't interested in the book. We're sunk.

I fasten his seat belt. He quickly skips past five stages of hysteria into paralysis and allows himself to be covered with an airline blanket. All that's sticking out are two huge eyes, the outside of his thumb-sucking fist, and a few shreds of Seewah.

We take off. Charlie opens his mouth and wails. The corner of our section of the plane sounds like an Irish wake. Around thirty-five thousand feet, the keening ceases and the catatonia resumes, to be interrupted only for the pointed question, at lunch, "Where's my hot dog?" When informed by the stewardess that the caterers managed to forget his food, he allows himself to be fed, like an infant, and chews a bite or two of rye bread and butter. Then he pops his thumb back into his mouth and falls asleep, mercifully, at 11:30 A.M. He hasn't slept at that hour since he was six months old.

When we get off the plane, he can hardly walk. His father carries him to the baggage area, and when he places Charlie on the ground, Charlie stands, rooted to the spot, like a statue. The child will not move a muscle.

An our after we have arrived at the hotel beach, all is fine again except for one teeny little problem: in a week we have to fly home.

"Do you think," I ask my husband, "that we could convince him it's Amtrak?"

Bermuda Shorts

WE have decided to take Charlie along on our vacation to Bermuda, basically because we have no choice. Either he comes along or we don't go. We sign up for seven diaper-changing days and six Bankie-Seewah nights. We study the faces of the staff in the brochures, looking for signs of a high degree of child tolerance.

Little do we know that by journey's end Charlie will be running the hotel and that "Brenuda," as he calls it, will be anxiously awaiting his return.

THE FOUR MINUTE MEAL

We are seated at our table in the dining room and are presented with the evening's menu.

Waterloo. Eight courses, served consecutively.

What to do? A quick conference between Mommy and Daddy. Charlie is squirming in his seat.

The waiter appears. "May I take your order for drinks?" He eyes Charlie. Charlie eyes him back.

Mommy and Daddy try to look supremely casual, sophisticated.

"We'd like to order everything now," Daddy says.
"And we'd like you to bring it all at once," Mommy adds.
"What?" the waiter says. Il ne comprend pas. We try again.
"Just bring *all* the courses at one time," we say pleasantly.
He shrugs. "You're sure?"
We nod. Charlie nods. We help him build a choo-choo out of ninety-nine metal cars we've brought to the dining room in a small tote bag.

Ten minutes later, the waiter staggers out with all our food. And while everyone else placidly sips their Bermuda Coolers, we feed Charlie cream of asparagus soup, roll and butter, lettuce with sauce, and a chicken leg.

By the end of our stay, the waiter has got it down pat. We're mainlining Maalox, and Charlie is supreme ruler of the dining room, the Only Child Who sits through His Meal. On our last night, dining room staffers line up to receive wet kisses from my son the prince.

THE CRUISEWEAR LINE

I have packed all of Charlie's good clothes—including his Bar Mitzvah outfit, purchased for his cousin's shindig—but I must say he is surpassed in this respect by the other Toddler-in-Residence. This child is the very model of fashion, from his green sun-visor down to the tips of his Day-Glo, neon-colored jellies. A veritable peacock, he and his outfits are a cause for comment among the other vacationing Mommies.

Some of his regalia includes:

- A black off-the-shoulder *Flashdance*-style sweatshirt, with gaping, torn holes, worn over black-and-white patterned shorts ("Couldn't they get him something without moths?" my husband inquires, unaware of how drop-dead chic all this is);

- A zebra-print bikini bathing suit with a Harry Truman-style Hawaiian shirt on top;

- High-top Harlem Globetrotters sneakers in flashing turquoise;

- Pastel sweat suits in clashing colors;

- Six pairs of coordinated suspenders to wear with his nighttime knee pants outfits.

Charlie looks like Tom Sawyer in his Oshkosh duds next to this little prince in his finery. I spend a lot of time wondering where these clothes have been purchased. No store I've ever been in carries things like these. Did they buy them in Soho? Noho? Boho?

The very worst part of all, however, is that this kid can also pronounce alligator much better than Charlie, who still struggles over his syllables.

"Do you think," I ask my husband, "that if we dressed Charlie differently, he'd talk better?"

"Sure," my husband replies. "With a lisp."

Oh.

Wish you were here

DEAR Grandma and Poppa,
    Charlie is having a wonderful time on his vacation. The man who sings calypso songs at the pool always does the song from *Annie* ("Tomorrow") whenever Charlie comes by to see him. Yesterday he gave Charlie a free cassette of his songs, as a present. The chambermaid who turns down the beds at night gives Charlie extra chocolates, and everyone who works at the hotel knows Charlie by name. They don't know us, however, unless we're with him. Then we're called "the people with Charlie." Charlie also has a lot of girlfriends, mostly older women. One is six-and-a-half and the other is thirty-two, on her honeymoon. She talked to Charlie for an hour at the pool yesterday.
    We think it might be nice to come here without Charlie for our own vacation one day, but we know it's not possible. They'd kill us if we didn't bring him.

                                        love and kisses
                                from the people with Charlie

Hamptons Diary by Charlie

This weekend much of the social whirl will be centered on Long Island..."The Joys of Summer '85' is the Guild Hall of East Hampton's second annual weekend of feasts—26 parties today and tomorrow at private homes all over the South Fork...."
—*The New York Times*, July 19, 1985

Drive out to the Hamptons in the red car. Along the road men are working with bulldozers and tractors. Hi bulldozers and tractors! I like the house. I can hear the railroad trains when they go by. Hi, trains!

... With tickets at $100 a person for each event, no one has yet made the whole circuit....

Every morning there are frogs in the swimming pool. Daddy catches them in the net. He lets me talk to the frogs. Hi, frogs! Ribbit-ribbit. When I ride to the beach, I see the farmers in the field on their tractors. Hi, farmers! Hi, tractors!

... The original invitation offered a choice of 41 parties, but some hosts had to cancel and some parties just didn't sell tickets. . . .

On the beach today a little boy had no bathing suit on. His mommy only had on half a bathing suit. My Daddy saw. Hi, lady!

. . . Not surprisingly, the people who support Guild Hall are mainly well-off homeowners from East Hampton and nearby communities. . . .

I lost my jellies on the beach and got mad because my sandloader isn't working right. I waved to the airplane flying over my head, close to the water. Hi, airplane!

. . . A totally unrelated event will be happening at the Guild Hall Museum tomorrow . . . a party after the preview for the likes of George Plimpton, Budd Schulberg, Kurt Vonnegut and Jill Krementz, Peter Maas, Morton Gottlieb, Sidney Lumet, Sheldon Harnick and Joseph Heller. . . .

Mommy and Daddy took me to a restaurant. I drew on the tablecloth with crayons. I had french fries and ketchup. We're leaving tomorrow. Bye, Hamptons!

Broken Grownups

Half a Mil and We'll Throw in the Kid

ON a summer Sunday, after two years of perusing real estate ads, we took the plunge and called some agents. Smelling blood, they pounced and in a twinkling had set up eight appointments.
"That's okay," I said breezily. "I've got a sitter all day Monday."
The sitter had a twenty-four-hour virus.
And that is how we ended up visiting eight apartments en famille, as it were. Which resulted in a rather classic confrontation. Boy versus co-op.
The first building was, shall we say, spiffy. Very moneyed lobby. Doorpeople who sniffed as they gave you the head-to-toe. We plunked down on an expensive couch in the tastefully refurbished lobby to wait. We stared at elevatormen. They stared back at us. Everyone was in gray uniforms. We tried to look Proper and Respectful. Right for the building.
Residents entered, singly and in groups. The co-op board among them, no doubt. And that's when Charlie made his move. First he decided to see what happened when you ran extremely fast and tried to skid on a marble floor while wearing Keds. Then he did his falling-down-on-the-ground number.
He crawled. We died. A nice little old lady, undoubtedly very rich and

most probably wife of the president of the building's board of directors, approached my son, at the moment writhing on his belly like a snake, as we snarled at him, sotto voce, "*Get up.*"

"Hello," came the Proper Nasal Tones of the people who never had to earn money a day in their lives. "What's your name?"

"Cocky sesstone," Charlie said brightly, doing his Jabberwock impression. We died some more.

By the time the agent had arrived, we had exposed a good 15 percent of the building's residents to the sight of Charlie's rear end, elevated in the air as he crawled like an Army recruit through the muck and slime of the training course. In their tastefully refurbished lobby. In full view of the plethora of uniformed building staff.

That was the first place.

Once inside an apartment, this one on Park Avenue no less, Charlie set his sights on having a good time. Boys just want to have fun. He headed straight for the child's room and silence descended.

The problem occurred when we had to leave. Charlie's now convinced that this apartment thing is just great, you get to go to a brand-new place with a whole lot of terrific stuff and *play* . . . until Mommy and Daddy want to leave, and then it's Tantrum City.

"Don' wanna go," Charlie wails.

We grit our teeth and try to smile sweetly at the real estate agent. She understands. Kids. But we're trying to make that Lasting Good Impression, and we are not amused.

Next apartment, saints preserve us, there's another kid's room as well as a living room populated by large sculptured versions of jungle animals. Whoopee. Charlie's faith in parental humanity is restored.

Then it's time to go. The volume of the shriek machine goes up two decibels. "Wanna stay in the apartment!"

"Quite a scream," the real estate agent observes politely.

"Can it," we address Charlie through gritted teeth. Edgar Bergen couldn't have done it with less lip motion.

Charlie gives his father a whack. We are rapidly approaching the point of no return, discipline-wise. What to do?

We breathe deeply and explain, patiently, reasonably (they don't want child abusers living in co-ops, do they?) that we are going to yet another apartment where there may (we pray to God) be another room with toys. And if he's a *really* good boy, Mommy and Daddy may even *buy* one of these apartments!

Charlie nods, tears glistening.

Next place isn't promising. A long hall. Then a door opens and out pops the head of a small boy. Bravo! Charlie spots the head, ascertains that where there's a boy there's a collection of toys, and makes a beeline for the door.

This time he departs like a gentleman. "We going to another apartment? We going to see some more toys? Want to find a new friend." It's going to be a cinch.

The next stop ends our run of luck. No toys, no child, only a woman psychiatrist with a schitzy dog. Some pop-eyed little Freudian breed. Charlie amuses himself by bombarding the beast with his miniature bulldozer. Do they allow dog abusers into co-ops either?

The afternoon is young, but Charlie is younger. Shall I compare thee to a three-year-old's day? He's just getting started. A further stop yields an even more paranoid dog who takes one look at my son and turns on the barkorama switch. We leave quickly.

Luckily we get a break at this juncture. We switch agents. Good-bye old worn-out one, hello new fresh one who might get to see Charlie in a different light. We wash his hands and face off with Daddy's handkerchief and some club soda.

This new agent is the mother of two sons. Their childhoods must be part of living memory, however; because the first thing she does is give Charlie a ballpoint pen to play with. Now we have to try to get it away before we visit the next place.

Of course he won't give it back. I have to barter. Charlie, like the Indians on Manhattan Island, will give anything away for a cheap and gaudy bauble. He exchanges his precious new pen for a stick of gum.

Which brings me to the climax of our story.

Entering the last of our apartments for the day, we note the stodginess of the building. Doormen frown; no one offers to give Charlie "five." When he falls down in *this* lobby, one look at the face on the elevatorman and he leaps to his feet at once. I'm beginning to wonder if I might not want to live here.

The co-op is owned by people of great culture, books, records, African masks everywhere, two silver foil-wrapped portions of pheasant defrosting atop the kitchen counter. We try to look Worldly and Welcome, as International as MasterCard. Charlie chomps on his gum and plays footsie with a King Charles spaniel. All goes swimmingly, and we exchange literary pleasantries as we bid the owners fond adieu.

We step into the corridor and ring for the elevator.

It is then that Charlie speaks up.

"Mommy, I left something," he says.

"Left what, dear?" I ask, wondering what defrosted pheasant tastes like.

"My gum."

"You left your GUM?" My voice goes up three octaves.

Daddy turns bright red. We bend toward Charlie. The real estate agent, smiling sweetly, intervenes.

"Why don't we go back and *find* it," she says, taking his arm.

I am by now absorbed in a vision of these eminently civilized people sitting down to their pheasant to discuss the nice little boy who just visited, comfortably perched atop a fresh wad of Trident sugarless bubble gum.

I can't exactly say the agents have been calling back in droves.

Big Bird on my Back

Of course you're aware that virtually all children between the ages of one and a half and five are hopelessly addicted *to Sesame Street.*
What you may not have realized is that Mommies and Daddies are, too. While the kids mainline the stuff regularly, parents find themselves helplessly drawn in and soon find their preoccupation overriding much of what formerly interested them.

Here's what has happened to cocktail party conversation as a result.

BEFORE:

"What do you think are the chances for Reagan's tax proposals passing this year?"
I think it's incredible how everyone who survives major plane crashes are smokers who sit in the back. Do you think there's a message there?"
"The president of my parent corporation wants everyone in an executive position to lose ten pounds. My secretary told me to cut off my head."
Isn't this fascinating?
But take these same human beings and give them small children for a year or so, then see what the same party chat has now become.

AFTER:

"Did you catch that episode on last week with Sally Ride taking off like a rocket?"
"I love the one where Robert MacNeil does his report on Mr. Snuffelupagus."
"There are at least seven different segments with Suzanne Farrell. The best one is when she dances Giselle and then eats yogurt."
"I'll bet you didn't know that was Ron Darling pitching to Big Bird last month!"

What eventually occurs is that your kid outgrows the show while your fascination continues, unabated. You're hooked. People have been known to have second children to disguise their addiction. Shut the TV off? And miss the time that everyone finally *sees* Snuffy at last? No way.

I'm thinking of starting a SesameEnders Clinic for parents to learn to kick the habit. You press a button that flips the audio of *Sesame Street* instantly over to the State of the Union Message.

Charlie Takes a Meeting

THE publishers want to meet Charlie.
We arrange a suitable date; not too near lunchtime in case he's hungry, not too early in the morning in case he's sleepy, not too late in the afternoon in case he's cranky.
 I decide that it's incumbent on me to explain a bit of the nature of this visit to my son.
 "Charlie, we're going to the publisher."
 "Publisher?" he repeats, wide-eyed. This is a new word.
 "Yes. They, uh . . ." I pause. What do they do? How do I explain this? I settle for the obvious, and wrong, explanation, "They make books," which I, as an author, know they most certainly do not. Only an author can make a book.
 He nods.
 "We're going to meet two editors," I say, not wanting to promise anything more like the head of the company or the CEO of the megaglomerate that owns the publishing house.
 Charlie nods complacently and resumes his backing-up garbage-truck noise.
 The day of The Meeting dawns warm and humid. I dress Charlie in an

outfit that's not-too-fancy, not-too-plain and pray that he won't fall in a mud puddle. The fact that there are no mud puddles around doesn't matter. They have a way of appearing at times like these.

We take a taxi (the bus might be dirty), and Charlie continues to ask where we're going. When we get out, he tells the cab driver we're "going to the publisher."

When we arrive, we're too early, so we take a walk. Each store we pass elicits the same response from Charlie:

Shoe store: "Is that the publisher?"
Drug store: "Is that the publisher?"
Irish bar: "Is that the publisher?"

Ignoring the irony in this, I tell him we'll soon be at a big building where, inside, he'll meet his bookmakers.

We go up on the elevator. Daddy meets us at the front desk. We eye each other nervously. Our glances ask the same question: Is this kid gonna screw it up? We sit and wait.

An editor finally emerges. Charlie is making one of his garbage-truck noises. Tentative "hellos" are exchanged. We are shown into her office. A repast is laid out on her desk, enough for five toddlers: a dozen homemade chocolate chip cookies, several containers of chocolate milk, a jug of apple cider. Supersnack.

The second editor appears. Charlie is utterly silent, playing with the swivel chair and twirling it around and around.

We make chat. Charlie refuses to respond to our gentlest suggestions. "Want to sing a song?" Zero. "Want to say your whole name?" Nope. "Want to count to twenty?" Are you kidding?

We knew this was going to happen. We talk to the editors more vivaciously than before, Making Up for the Kid.

Fifteen long minutes pass. Charlie has spilled apple cider on his white shirt and on Mommy (natch) and has eaten one-half of one cookie. Now he is lying on the floor making na-na noises. Where are the smart remarks, the epigrams, the Charlie charm? Hold the *People* magazine interview, folks, the *Good Morning America* slot. What we've got on our hands is . . . a dud.

The editors can only praise his forbearance. How nicely he's behaving, how he isn't running around and pestering us and interrupting. I'm thinking, if only he'd interrupt. He's still alternately twirling the chair or lying on the floor.

He rouses himself briefly to color a picture with markers. He announces that it's a swing. A broken swing. Okay, I'll take that. But then he's lying on the floor again, na-na-na-na.

I am bathed in flop sweat.

They're going to cancel the book contract and ask for their money back.

They are convinced I'm a Mommy-liar and am making all of this up. Typical of all bragging Mommies, right?

Mercifully the meeting ends. We leave. "Say good-bye, Charlie," we prompt tonelessly.

As soon as we get into the taxi to go home, no, as soon as we hit the street, Charlie springs to life. "Look, look," he cries, and soon he's jabbering on about what's happening out there in his big, bad, noisy old world. The chatterbox *redux*.

I stare at the apple cider stains on my dress and wonder if it might not have been better to pretend I had made it all up and that Charlie's antics weren't real. Now they're going to call my book fiction and market it on the same shelf as Sidney Sheldon and Judith Krantz. We could call it I *Fantasized My Child Wasn't a Zombie*.

Do you think he did it on purpose?

The Littlest Prince

ROYALTY holds a fascination for Americans, but in our household there is a particular enchantment with Prince William, the heir to the heir to the British throne. His highness's birthday falls a scant few days after *our* little prince's (thus, when Princess Diana was throwing up with morning sickness, I was, too), and there's a faint resemblance there in terms of hair color, build, general little-boyishness. In fact, when William made an appearance on a recent TV interview with Mom and Dad and Baby Brother, Charlie was delighted by his antics.

Which got me to thinking. They could be great pals, these two. Suppose the next time the royal folk visit our shores they bring the kids. And just suppose we could arrange a play date for Charlie with Prince William. Wouldn't that be neat?

I'm sure it would go something like this:

Ding-dong, goes our doorbell, after the doorman has buzzed them up ("There's a prince and three bodyguards and a nanny down here for Master Charles"). Charlie, as usual, rushes to the door. I try to yank up his high socks, having dressed him in short pants. Prince William always wears short pants, I've noticed. We have worked on the bowing bit, but I don't think it's going to happen.

Prince William toddles in with his entourage, and of course Charlie does not bow. He falls on the floor, in a heap, which is what he always does when company comes. Then he grabs away his new bike and gives the prince a shove. The bodyguards come running over at once, but I intervene and explain sweetly that *Mommy* will tell Charlie that he's not to push anybody. Ever.

   We offer milk and Chewy Chips Ahoy. Nanny mumbles something about biscuits. William settles for a Jell-O pudding pop. He asks where Charlie's servants are and is this a palace? I graciously explain that Charlie's Mommy and Daddy are on active duty at all times and that nobody in America has a palace except for Harry and Leona Helmsley and maybe Hugh Hefner.

   Diana shows up two hours late to pick up the kid, and I try not to act pissed. She informs me brusquely that William is rarely allowed sugar treats and that the Jell-O Pop will cause him to miss his nap. Another day, another Mommy. I'm dying to ask her where to get designer fashions at a discount in London, but I don't want to be pushy.

   So that's it, my fantasy. Which only goes to prove about as absolutely as anything could that play dates are the most boring way to spend your time in the whole world, I don't care who the kid or the Mommy is.

Sesame Street as a Metaphor for Life

And that's the Way it is

This is a really stinky world, as all you avid news hounds know only too well. Every night the news is bad, getting worse, with no respite in sight. Whatever happened to all that Happy News? If you live with Charlie, avid consumer of Gold*fish News*, you get a far nicer fix on reality, mainly because Charlie's version is a lot better than what's really going on.

For instance, in New York City there was a terrible accident when a crane toppled over and pinned a woman beneath, causing screaming headlines for days. When Charlie saw the television film of the accident, he wanted to know exactly what was going on.

"It's a crane," I started to explain. I was going to have to tell him something, because from now on, I would have to give all cranes an extremely wide berth, and I wanted Charlie to know there was danger here.

He was staring at the screen, fascinated by the tangle of metal.

"It fell down and hurt someone," I said.

"It's a bad crane," said Charlie. "It's broken. They going to get a new one?"

Right. I could see the headlines in the New York Post: BAD CRANE BROKEN, MOMMY GOES TO STORE TO BUY NEW ONE.

Reagan is another favorite subject for Charlie's philosophizing, probably because he's such a familiar face on *Goldfish News*. When the whole flap about the Bitburg Cemetery visit took place, Charlie listened avidly to panel discussions and commentators arguing endlessly about the President's plans. I couldn't understand Charlie's interest until he turned away from the set to offer his editorial view:

"Mommy," he said excitedly. "Reagan's going to visit Big Bird!"

Sure he is. And he's going to be accompanied by Oscar the Grouch (Pat Buchanan), Cookie Monster (Donald Regan), Ernie (George Schultz), and Bert (Larry Speakes).

And if Charlie sees anyone crying or unhappy on the news (convicted murderers sentenced to the electric chair, families of victims of famine or flood, angry denizens of crime-ridden neighborhoods), he simply rushes into his room and brings them a present.

"Here," he says to the person on the TV. "Don't cry, it's a birthday present." Then he sings "Happy Birthday" at top speed and pretends to blow out the candles on a cake.

I wonder if Walter Cronkite got started this way.

Hoping your news is good news, Good Night!

A Generation of Social Workers

THE pressure is on for toddlers to succeed in their early years so as to ensure a place of prominence in the future. They are to become business magnates, Nobel-winning doctors, lawyer-advisers to presidents or vastly overeducated rock stars who act like boors publicly but who can complete *The New York* Times crossword puzzle in four minutes flat. In ink.

I'm sorry, then, to have to report that an upswelling of sixties-like empathy among the Baby Boom Babies could lead to a completely different picture: pampered children will rebel by occupying the office of an Ivy League dean and smoking his cigars; rioters will alternately protest against "injustice" and uphold "peace" and "love."

How do I know this? Listen:

At a fairly posh birthday party not long ago, a group of expensively groomed children was half watching a puppet show. The subject was *The Three Bears*, and the puppeteer, to jazz up his version, improvised a series of skits during which Goldilocks perched precariously atop a series of bear chairs. Attention waned among the partygoers until the Goldilocks puppet plummeted from the chair to the bottom of the stage and whacked her head with a resounding thunk.

The children gasped, collectively, and riveted their attention on the puppet. The puppeteer, sensing their heightened interest, asked, "Does anyone want to come up and kiss Goldilocks's head and make her all better?"

The stage was stampeded. No one could wait. The falling-down scene had to be repeated three times to accommodate all those eager head kissers.

Now I ask you, are these children demonstrating the kind of Type A behavior that parents seem so intent on instilling in their tots?

Nope.

Will these kids ruthlessly battle their way to the top of their nursery school classes, never mind whose heads they're stepping on, in order to achieve fame and fortune by the age of five? Not to mention a thorough proficiency with a Commodore 64?

I'm beginning to wonder. . . .

Then what, you ask, is the final word on all this pressure, anxiety, jockeying for position, and generally tense competitiveness of late that swirls around very small children?

Parents.

White Flight

I really had no idea what I was getting into when I got pregnant. I'm not speaking of the physical aspects of having a baby nor of the time, energy, and expense involved. I am referring to the scramble to Get Your Child into the Right School.

I was aware of the private school problem, certainly, and had heard about parents of five-year-olds sweating out the decision. People told me how they got letters from their senators attesting to the child's promise as a kindergartener. It had been reported that many hearts had been broken in this quest for education.

It wasn't all that impressive, I thought. You had five years before the problem reared its ugly head. Five years you could enjoy and savor.

Not so fast.

I did not know that all of this has now percolated down to the teenies and that Charlie was just the right age to be stuck right in the middle of . . . Nursery School Fever.

I know they sign them up for school in England when they're born, but it's a bit silly to be wheeling around a six-month-old and to be asked where you're planning to apply next year. You look down at your baby's chubby bowlegs and wonder if he'll ever walk, let alone say a few words. And here's some mother trying to tell you where you should be calling for applications? The idea is so ridiculous. It's like filling out an application for a college education for a fetus. There's no *reality*. Aren't you supposed to have some idea what your child is like as a person before you send him to school? All I knew about Charlie was that if given half the chance, he'd swallow large chunks of *The New Yorker*.

Even stranger things began happening:

- Letters arrived in the mail asking if I, as a responsible parent, wanted to prepare my child properly for the crucible that was Life. Specifically, would my child Make It? The letter writer was offering instruction on teaching my child testing and interview skills so he'd give the correct impression. I threw these letters away. Should I have saved them?

- Mommies asked me more frequently if I knew where I was applying for nursery school. Since I am of a practical nature and nothing if not truly lazy, I'd reply, "Across the street," which wasn't far from the truth, since there is a school across from us. But the shock expressed on the Mommies' faces told me I had the wrong attitude. Was Charlie going to miss out on something, even though he wasn't yet one year old?

- When I finally did apply for school, I sent in only one application. The school, lovely and nurturing, was close to home and seemed removed from the competitive push of the places the Mommies wanted. I figured we'd probably get in, since it seemed like such a quiet haven. But an encounter with one of Charlie's park pals gave me great pause. The little boy, Evan, was with his caregiver. Where had Evan applied, I asked. The caregiver didn't know the names of the schools, but she knew the number. "Twelve places." And I had applied to one. What if Charlie didn't get in?

- At our interview, the lovely head of the school tells us that nearly 150 families have applied for places in her school. So much for quiet little neighborhood haven. I am reminded of the 520 neurotic college applcants from my high school graduating class. Many never made their third-choice schools, let alone their first or second. A lot of disappointed people went to Adelphi that year. Would Charlie suffer the same fate, at the tender age of eighteen months?

- We get in. Ecstasy. He's set for three years. Then we have to go through this again. It's enough to make you want to move to the suburbs. And yet we are not through, because all around us, par ents are churning through the system. Not content with one school, they are pulling their children out after a year and going someplace else, one of the bigger, fancier, "name" schools. What's going on? At the end of Charlie's first year of nursery school, 75 percent of his class is moving. Crazed Mommies and Daddies cannot leave well enough alone. By the age of eighteen, many of these children will have been in as many as six different schools.

I have dubbed this activity White Flight because of its short sighted, prejudiced quality and its equally blind movement in one direction, *away*. Apparently it is happening all over, symptomatic of this kind of parental anxiety that used to be confined to things like making sure you had a good orthodontist or that shoes fit really well. But discarding schools like scarcely worn shoes is misguided and only makes the turmoil occurring in the system worse. Added to the pool of new applicants are all those being transferred.

The worst part is that these little kids are so very nice and seem to enjoy themselves at almost any school.

And Evan and his twelve applications? The caregiver recently informed me that since he did not make his "first-choice" school, they are keeping him out one more year and trying again next fall. They are going to go through the whole process and reapply. Twelve more times.

The Official Rotten Mommy Test

ARE you a Rotten Mommy? Place a check mark next to the *best* answer. Use number two soft-lead pencils ONLY. Do not turn to the answer sheet until you have completed the entire questionnaire.

1. You enter the local stationery store to buy Father's Day cards. You take your toddler. When you refuse to buy your child a six-foot-tall turquoise stuffed Smurf (even though it's been reduced from $325 to $59.95), your child has a tantrum. You

   a. leave the store immediately and neglect to buy your husband his Father's Day card, leading to a major fight and no sex;
   b. give the kid a pinch on the upper arm, bend low and whisper, "One more sound out of you and I'm going to make you watch Regis Philbin every morning";
   c. try to reason with your child, explaining the rules for good, positive social interaction and how this behavior disrupts the workings of free enterprise;

d. Deny.

2. In the supermarket you give your kid a bag of potato chips to ensure peace and quiet. This is followed by demands for Crunchy Cheez Doodles, Double Stuf Oreos, Butter-Twist Pretzels, etc. When you refuse, your kid's mouth opens and out comes the Scream of the Century. Activity in the store comes to a dead halt, rather like the TV commercials when people confide, "My broker is E. F. Hutton, and E. F. Hutton says . . ." A pin can be heard dropping. You

   a. remind your child that one treat is the limit, period;
   b. raise your hand and threaten to issue forth a good smack;
   c. take this time to have a serious talk with your child, explaining the rules for being in public, shopping, going out with Mommy, etc.
   d. Deny.

3. Your kid decks his friend when fighting over a toy. You

   a. immediately remove him from the scene and have a serious talk explaining the rules for playing with other children;
   b. deck your kid;
   c. trade your kid in for another model;
   d. Deny.

4. Your child, in a fit of beastly overpossessiveness, refuses to share his or your presence with another person in an elevator. As soon as someone else gets on, it's Tantrum time. You

   a. stop riding in elevators and take the stairs;
   b. have a serious talk, explaining the rules for riding in elevators;
   c. tell the child that when he or she grows up to become Nelson Rockefeller or Gloria Vanderbilt a private elevator will be possible.
   d. Deny.

CORRECT ANSWERS:

1. Deny. You could say, "This is not my kid."
2. Deny. Try, "Does anybody know whose kid this is?"
3. Deny. "Yoo-hoo, did someone misplace a small child?"
4. Deny. "I'm just the babysitter/caregiver/ housekeeper/cousin-from-out-of-town. The mother works full-time."

(Note: On completion of the *verbal* portion of your RMTs, you may now go on to complete your *math* section. You will be asked to complete various sets of equations, such as "If X equals the price of a set of Lego blocks and Y equals the number of sets on the market, how many hours will it take Mommy to pick all of them up off the floor, not counting the number stashed behind the couch pillows?" Good luck!)

Afterword: Do Daddies Make the best Mommies?

by Charlie's Daddy

ALTHOUGH I am Charlie's biological father, I sometimes get confused about my role and catch myself thinking that I actually am his mommy. For instance, when I return with him from an outing in the playground, I tell my wife about some of the things I learned from "the other mothers."

I have learned that I am not the only father who thinks this way, and that—thanks to the emergence of sexual parity in the modern world—many husbands find themselves in competition with their wives for honors in motherhood. Some fathers consider themselves the equals of their children's mothers in many respects, and their superiors in several categories. I must confess I am not above such feelings. Let me give you some examples.

- *Pushing Strollers.* While I'm sure a great deal of scientific thought has gone into the design of strollers, it is obvious from a glance that anybody who pushes her child in a stroller daily for one month will have a back shaped like a sickle and shins lacerated beyond the competence of modern medicine to restore. Yet mommies never deviate from Standard Strolling

Posture, slumped behind the vehicle with both hands on the handlebars, taking itty-bitty Madame Butterfly steps so that their ankles will not bang against the frame.

It took me but a single stroll with Charlie to determine that there is a better way. The way is to walk to the left of the carriage, pushing the port handlebar with your right hand (reverse the position if you are a lefty). By applying thrust at approximately a forty-five-degree angle, you can propel the stroller forward in full stride.

Another thing is that mommies have never figured out how to go through a door pushing a stroller. They lean over their child's head and push the door mightily to keep it from swinging shut on the kid, during which moment they ram the stroller through the opening, taking the full brunt of the slamming door on their triceps or hipbones. Any father, after one trial and one error, will perceive that the proper approach is to turn the stroller around and pull it backward through the door.

Mommies also have little sense of the relationship between the weight of a shopping bag loaded with four sixty-four-ounce bottles of apple juice over the handles of a stroller and a twenty-five-pound child sitting on the stroller seat, as has been demonstrated by countless instances of kids being catapulted onto their heads by mommies ignoring fundamental stroller physics.

- *Spanking.* Mommies are good threateners, but they are rotten spankers. They plead, reason, negotiate, cajole, warn, and manipulate guilt, but when it comes to the application of corporal punishment, most mommies are abject cream puffs.

Charlie's mommy uses the same amount of brute force to punish her son as she does to fold meringue. Mommies do not come from the school of child rearing that holds that children are savages whose wills must be broken if they are not to tear through the social fabric like crazed beasts.

We knew from dog training that the undisciplined animal responds best to loud noises. Unfortunately, the sound of Mommy's hand on Charlie's Pamper-padded behind is approximately that of turning the pages of *The Wall Street Journal* in a library.

The resounding thwack of an open hand on the gluteal portion of a child's anatomy is both satisfying to the parent and educational for the miscreant. I happen to know because I did it to Charles—once. Ten minutes later the imprint of my fingers was still visible in the form of four roseate ovals on his right buttock. Whereupon I rushed him to the toy department of Gimbel's East to make restitution with a dump truck, a forklift, a front loader, and a road grader of sufficient size and cost to renovate the West Side Highway. I don't understand: it worked for the fourth-form masters in *Tom Brown's School*

Days. I guess I just lack the requisite sadism.

Except when it comes to . . .

- *Tickling*. Mommies don't know beans about tickling. They employ a kind of feathery motion with their fingers like somebody playing a Chopin nocturne on the piano, and they warble "Koochy-koochy-koochy" as they perform this pathetic operation. No wonder it elicits little more than wan smiles from their children. Proper tickling requires you to dig your thumb •nd to keep it there far beyond the limits of human endurance. Then there's Pfuffing the Belly, which you perpetrate by inhaling to full capacity, pressing your mouth just upside the belly button, and trumpeting like the Angel of Doom while rooting about with your nose like a pig that's detected a truffle. Koochy-koochy indeed. Gimme a break!

- *Playing*. A corollary of the above is that mommies are not very good at playing with their children. Their problem is that they feel sorry for them and let them win all the time.

I can see no good whatever coming out of letting your kids beat you. It gives them a distorted picture of the Real World and promotes infantilism, and no three-year-old of mine is going to be accused of infantilism if I have anything to say about it. My attitude is, play to win, no quarter asked and none given. From my viewpoint, the best measure of successful play with your kid is whether he remembers it in therapy forty years later during his mid-life crisis. If you play Hide and Seek, hide where it will be impossible for your kid to find you—like the appliances floor of Macy's Department Store or the mezzanine of the Metropolitan Opera House during intermission. If you are playing catch with your child, smoke him with a fastball clocked at ninety-six miles per hour. If you play Wiffle Ball, brush him back with a couple of high hard ones.

Children whose parents need to win often resort to cheating, so keep a sharp eye out for that. If your kid cheats you, cheat back. And if he complains to Mommy, you know what to say: "*He* started it!"

- *Shopping*. Mommies don't understand the purpose of shopping with their children. The purpose of shopping with children is Having Fun with Shopping Carts. Mommies just don't appreciate what spectacular vehicles shopping carts are. With a running start and no crotchety pensioners obstructing the aisle, a well-launched shopping cart can achieve speeds up to fifteen miles on a straightaway. The little treadmill at the cash register is another fun ride unless you get a checkout person with no sense of humor.

Another complaint I have is that mommies follow a shopping list and never depart from it. How dull! The only way to shop is to throw into the cart everything your kid points to, and while you're at it to drop a few items of your own in there like tahini or sun-dried tomatoes that will remain in your larder until life as we have known it ceases to exist.

- *Loving.* When it comes to loving their kids, I am convinced that daddies are every bit the equals of mommies. At least, I cannot imagine that anybody could love a kid more than I love mine. Why is it, then, that when Charlie is scared, he asks for Mommy? When he's hurt, he asks for Mommy? When he's confused, he asks for Mommy?

I suppose, for the same reason I do.

Leslie Tonner is the author of eight books, both fiction and non-fiction. She and her family live in Manhattan.

INTEGRATED MEDIA

Open Road Integrated Media is a digital publisher and multimedia content company. Open Road creates connections between authors and their audiences by marketing its ebooks through a new proprietary online platform, which uses premium video content and social media.

Videos, Archival Documents, and New Releases

Sign up for the Open Road Media newsletter and get news delivered straight to your inbox.

Sign up now at
www.openroadmedia.com/newsletters

FIND OUT MORE AT
WWW.OPENROADMEDIA.COM

FOLLOW US:
@openroadmedia and
Facebook.com/OpenRoadMedia

www.ingramcontent.com/pod-product-compliance
Lightning Source LLC
LaVergne TN
LVHW041626070426
835507LV00008B/465